Enacting the Sacrament

Enacting the Sacrament

Counter-Lollardy in the Towneley Cycle

Lauren Lepow

Rutherford • Madison • Teaneck
Fairleigh Dickinson University Press
London and Toronto: Associated University Presses

PR
644
.T6
L46
1990

Associated University Presses
440 Forsgate Drive
Cranbury, NJ 08512

Associated University Presses
25 Sicilian Avenue
London WC1A 2QH, England

Associated University Presses
P.O. Box 39, Clarkson Pstl. Stn.
Mississauga, Ontario
Canada L5J 3X9

The paper used in this publication meets the requirements
of the American National Standard for Permanence of Paper
for Printed Library Materials Z39.48-1984.

Library of Congress Cataloging-in-Publication Data

Lepow, Lauren Ethel.
  Enacting the Sacrament : counter-Lollardy in the Towneley cycle /
Lauren Lepow.
    p.   cm.
  Includes bibliographical references and index.
  ISBN 0-8386-3368-4 (alk. paper)
  1. Towneley plays.   2. Mysteries and miracle-plays.   English-
-History and criticism.   3. Sacraments in literature.   4. Lollards
in literature.   I. Title.
  PR644.T6L46   1990
  822'.051609—dc20   90-55003
                                                                 CIP

To

Martha L. Lepow

and to the memory of

Irwin H. Lepow

Contents

Acknowledgments

My coauthors are the many people who have taught me, argued with me, and encouraged me. Thomas Jambeck, Bennett Brockman, and Charles Owen conducted the fine seminars that awakened my interest in the literature of medieval England; they guided me through the doctoral dissertation in which I first began to explore sacramental reference in the Towneley plays. It was Jack Davis who asked me whether anything in the contemporary social or religious climate could explain the plays' insistent hammering away at what were surely theological truisms. That question led me to a closer look at John Wyclif and the Lollard heresy and to the conception of this study.

My other debts are numerous. Portions of chapters 5 and 6 of this study, in an earlier form, appeared in *Philological Quarterly*, whose permission to incorporate the material here I gratefully acknowledge. Marcia Dalbey provided much optimistic encouragement. Theresa Coletti generously read two earlier drafts of the study and offered a great many valuable suggestions for its improvement. My thanks also to Harry Keyishian, Julien Yoseloff, and Michael Koy, and to Beth Gianfagna, my editorial mentor. Cynthia Crumrine's intelligent and meticulous copyediting eliminated many errors and infelicities.

My greatest debt is to my husband, Michael Montgomery. Mike's knowledge and skills as an academic reference librarian have opened to me many avenues of inquiry through which this study has been deepened and enriched. More important than his librarianship has been his companionship and his belief in me and in this project. I thank him and our children, Thomas and Jean, for so graciously opening their home to the medieval world.

Introduction

As students of the English Corpus Christi cycles know, the relationship between these plays and the Church feast for which they are named has not always been deemed significant or, indeed, even existent. However, criticism of recent decades has leaned more and more on the assumption that the cycles shared social and doctrinal emphases inherent in the celebration of the feast, and the resulting studies have illuminated a great many complexities in the plays' content, organization, and dramatic and didactic effectiveness.

It is generally agreed that to understand these plays, we are well advised to learn everything we can about late medieval attitudes toward the Feast of Corpus Christi, its modes of celebration, and the Eucharistic sacrament that it honored. Scholars have demonstrated insistent Eucharistic reference in many component cycle plays and have tied it to the Corpus Christi occasion. Yet there is one question that has been explored only incompletely and that deserves renewed attention. One way of phrasing it is, Why were such plays, with such doctrinal emphases, necessary? Did not everybody have at least a rudimentary grounding in sacramental theology and—more important—an unshakable belief in Christ's Real Presence in the Eucharist? The answer, of course, is no.

As attested to by the period's proliferation of devotional manuals for the laity and, indeed, how-to books for the parish priest, the assumption of basic, catechismal knowledge in the community of late medieval English Christians was not made by the Church itself and should not be made by the modern student. There was room, plenty of room, for such educative devotional media as the Corpus Christi plays. But what of the other half of the question, that of the consensus of sacramental piety? Here too the historical answer is clear. Although the dating of the plays is still a controversial matter, it is most likely that their early coalescence overlapped the period of intense heretical activity in late fourteenth- and early fifteenth-century England. The plays and

Lollardy—the heretical movement that grew out of the teachings of John Wyclif—were historical bedfellows.

But by no means amicable ones. The sacrament exalted by the Corpus Christ feast—an exaltation echoed in, of the extant cycles, Towneley and N-Town—was at the center of Lollard antipathy to Church belief and practice. Lollardy was, among other things, an anticlerical and antisacramental movement that earned greatest opprobrium when it denied the doctrine of the Real Presence—denied, that is, that by transubstantiation Christ was actually made present in the sacramental species at each and every Mass. Are the plays—specifically the Towneley plays,[1] the focus of this study—aware of Lollardy? Do they respond to it? How? These are the questions this study is designed to approach.

Approach—not answer. Intentional fallacy aside, we cannot know what the Towneley playwrights and revisers were thinking about when they crafted these dramatic works; indeed, we do not know, and may never know, who they were. I readily concede that it is not possible to prove, however much I may privately incline to this view, that the Towneley cycle was in any way designed specifically to counter Lollardy as it fortified the spectators in orthodox belief. My intention is, rather, to explore a hypothesis that, while it is not susceptible of proof, may nonetheless lead to valuable insights about the cycle and its component plays. That is, aspects of the plays' language, themes, and organization may be examined as possible embodiments of counter-Lollard force. We cannot know whether that force was deliberately put there by the playwrights; we can speculate, however, on how these aspects may have been seen and felt by a spectator aware of or even leaning toward Lollard teachings. And these speculations can lead us toward a new gestalt of the cycle, its "meaning" for an imaginable and historically significant group within its original audience.

It is certain that no one "meaning" can be attached to the Towneley cycle or to any of its components. In a cogent discussion of how each enacted episode of a cycle served to evoke the entire cycle-frame *as held in the spectator's mind*, David Mills indirectly attests to the dramas' polysemy: he points out that what we know to be true of modern audiences is also relevant to their medieval counterparts; they "select what they will watch, with what degree of attention, and for how long. It is for them to relate as they will the performed part, the play, to the conceptual whole, the cycle-frame, held in their mind."[2] I am imagining a spectator who, eagerly or nervously, would scrutinize the plays for orthodox responses to Lollardy. I am imagining, too, that this spectator was one of a considerable number who were threatened or tempted by Lollardy: a movement that attacked the status quo, that was branded as heresy and could lead to death by fire—and that was also undeniably attractive in its stance against clerical corruption and its elevation of the individual to what orthodoxy deemed the purview of the priest alone. It is the "cycle-frame" as it took shape in the minds of such spectators as these that this study seeks to reconstitute.

Part 1, "Orthodoxy and Lollardy," establishes historical and theological reasons why the cycle *could* have served as a counter-Lollard force. It examines the relationship, actual and imaginable, between Lollardy and drama, and it explores the combating orthodox and Lollard theologies of God's Word and of the Eucharist. Specifically, I will seek to demonstrate how the Church saw its own creed and ritual and, in particular, its chief sacrament as an answer to Lollardy. Where the Lollards called for reliance on the Word of God in *scriptura sola*, the orthodox position was that the Word must be sought and engaged with not just in the Bible but also in priestly authority and ecclesiastical ritual—above all, in the Eucharist, where Word was daily made flesh for the sustenance of the worshipers. Lollardy was, to be sure, no mere set of cut-and-dried theological propositions; it was a complex (and internally varied) movement, whose social dimensions were as significant as its religious ones. Nor were the cycles mere repositories of dogma; they too were complex social phenomena. My focus on theology does not mean to deny these truths.[3] However, my central interest in this study is the way in which the theology embedded and dramatized in the Towneley cycle *answered* the theological stances of Lollardy. That this countering activity had broader dimensions which transcended Scholastic argumentation I have no doubt and will at times suggest quite specifically. In part 2, "The Cycle Enacts the Sacrament," I turn at length to the Towneley plays themselves, identifying their counter-Lollard elements and constructing an image of the "counter-Lollard cycle" that some part of the original audience is likely to have seen. By enacting the sacrament, I will suggest, the cycle responds to Lollardy as it illuminates and vitalizes the orthodox ritual, sharpening the spectators' desire for Eucharistic participation and their belief in its salvific primacy.

* * *

The ground I am exploring here is by no means untrodden. Two previous studies have focused directly on the Towneley cycle in the context of Lollard heresy. The earlier is Harold Patrick Brent's unpublished doctoral dissertation, "Authority and Heresy in the Towneley Cycle—Structure as Reflection of Theme" (University of Wisconsin, 1973). Brent argues that the cycle embodies antiauthoritarian social criticism: that its authors, particularly the Wakefield Master, align themselves with the period's heretics. Critical of this view is Theodore Richard DeWelles in his own dissertation, "The Social and Political Content of the Towneley Cycle" (University of Toronto, 1981). DeWelles perceives the Wakefield Master as a highly orthodox writer who wishes to reinforce Christian communal ideals in the face of the period's prevailing tendency toward materialism and individualism. The dramatist, DeWelles believes, is critical of the revolutionary peasant and the lawless noble alike. And while the playwright is by no means in sympathy with Lollardy, DeWelles finds him critical of the Church's excesses in its persecution of supposed Lollards.[4] Both of these scholars provide important insights into the sociopolitical world in which the Towneley cycle came into being. My study, however, diverges from theirs in emphasis as well as in conclusions: it focuses primarily on the theological differences between the orthodox Church and Lollardy; it concludes that the plays and the heretics were in this regard diametrically opposed.

Several broader published studies also provide significant foundations to the exploration undertaken here. To begin, there is the line of inquiry pursued in, for example, Russell Fraser's *The War against Poetry* and Jonas Barish's *The Antitheatrical Prejudice*.[5] In the earlier of these two studies, Fraser considers the stance of the late sixteenth-century polemicists against the drama: "The source of this animus is the delight in Naked Truth: the thing itself, undefiled, unaccoutered, for which the playwright or the vulgar empiric substitute their specious approximations." Fraser glances back to the medieval antecedents of these Renaissance warriors against poetry and finds chief among them the Lollard author of a tract known as *A Tretise of Miraclis Pleyinge*, whose targets undoubtedly included the Corpus Christi plays. Of this writer Fraser says, "What the preacher requires is a kind of abstract art, which is ideally no art at all, 'but as nakid lettris to a clerk to reden the truthe.'"[6]

The Lollard would see the drama as inimical to the Christian's engagement with the Word of God; but his was a minority view, and the orthodox Church had long tolerated and often supported religious plays. Barish traces this dichotomy to its roots in the contrasting theologies of Augustine and Tertullian. Tertullian's attitude toward mimesis, Platonist in flavor, was thoroughly disapproving: simply put, that which gratifies the senses distracts the Christian from matters of the spirit. Augustine, by contrast, promulgated "a theory [of mimesis] that appreciates the mimetic and spectacular elements in Christian worship itself, and allows for differences in value depending on the differing objects of imitation."[7] When Barish comes to the consideration of the Lollard *Tretise*, he perceives it as reverting from the established Augustinian tolerance "to the fierce fundamentalism of Tertullian"; the author "will admit of no form of mediation between the scriptural episode itself and the believer's spirit—no mediation except, presumably, such sermons as his own and those of his colleagues, which didactically expound the meaning of the episode in question."[8] The author of the *Tretise*, as Barish points out, is well aware that the plays enjoy considerable approbation; he recognizes a powerful rival. The power lies in large part in the plays' "intense immediacy, everything about them that makes them capable of stirring their audiences, . . . which in the preacher's jaundiced eye turns them into something abominable and sinister." Barish pertinently connects the Lollards' antitheatricalism with their antiliturgicalism and antisacramentalism.[9] The mimetic power of the plays and of the Mass were one and the same, a power that would lead the Christian—in the Lollard view—not toward God but down the garden path.

The most important examination of the relationship between Lollardy and drama is found in Ritchie D. Kendall's 1986 study, *The Drama of Dissent*.[10] Kendall differs from Barish and Fraser in finding religious dissenters—the Lollards included—not absolutely hostile to drama, but strikingly ambivalent and manifesting a complex aesthetic stance. Lollards did find the dramatic aesthetic experience spiritually dangerous; but, as Kendall points out, antitheatrical tracts, including the *Tretise*, are themselves "dramatic in form." Can one doubt the flattery inherent in imitation? Indeed, as Kendall's study demonstrates, the Lollards and the orthodox had quite a bit in common. For one thing, "the medieval dramatist and the itinerant Lollard preacher vied for the loyalties of much the same audience." Further, Kendall focuses on "the degree to which the Lollard sensibility was compatible with the aesthetic and religious principles of contemporary drama and the extent to which the Lollard felt compelled to generate his own theatrical conventions in order to give voice to the drama of his spiritual life."[11] For Lollardy and orthodoxy, the desired ends were the same—to reach communion with God's Word—but their means differed in crucial ways. The Lollard God was a far more remote entity and had to be approached by quite different avenues. Kendall speaks of the Lollards' "displacement of one idea of sacrifice with another" and their "attempt to substitute the ritual of biblical exegesis for that of the Eucharist."[12] Of the relationship between Lollardy and Corpus Christi drama, Kendall says pointedly, "That the cycles gave voice, eloquent voice, to a vision of Christian life alien to Lollardy is undeniable."[13]

The ideas informing Kendall's book and those by Fraser and Barish will recur in the pages to follow, particularly in those sections of part 1 in which I examine more closely Lollardy's attitudes toward drama and toward the orthodox positions from which the Lollards dissented. But in the remainder of the study my concern will be the reciprocal, namely, the drama's attitudes toward Lollardy: specifically, the counter-Lollardy of the Towneley cycle.

Enacting the Sacrament

Part 1
Orthodoxy and Lollardy

1
Lollardy and Drama

The vast and compelling popular drama of the Corpus Christi cycles held sway in England for nearly two centuries. Clerical authorship, town support, and guild production combined to create a spectacular annual expression of orthodox devotion, beginning in the late fourteenth century. Significantly, the cycles' demise must be attributed, at least in part, to orthodoxy as well—the Reformation's new orthodoxy that, in the later sixteenth century, underlay the plays' suppression.[1] The Corpus Christi cycles' theology has been explored by a number of insightful scholars who have documented its sophistication as well as its doctrinal purity. It is the purpose of this study to extend that exploration in a new direction. During the late fourteenth and fifteenth centuries, the English church was assailed by heresy, and some of its most cherished tenets were brought into question. The tensions generated by heresy affected members of all the Three Estates, and the plays written and performed during this period may be profitably analyzed in the context of these tensions.

Unlike her continental neighbors, England was largely untroubled by heresy until late in the Middle Ages. Indeed it may be said that her first heretic of note was the wellspring of Lollardy, John Wyclif (d. 1384), the Oxford Scholastic turned reformer. When Wyclif's heterodox doctrines found a popular audience in the 1380s—the period during which the cycles began to thrive[2]—a heretical movement grew rapidly. It is true that defining Lollardy as a "movement" is problematic in that neither its leadership nor its program can be articulated absolutely. The word *Lollard* eventually became a generic term for "heretic"—or anyone with whom one disagreed. However, Wyclif was surely the spiritual father of those who first came to be known as Lollards. He denied the doctrine of transubstantiation, and he believed in dominion by grace alone, not by earthly authority; he argued for the disendowment of the Church. These antisacra-

21

mental and anticlerical, antihierarchical views were central to his followers' beliefs. When, in 1382, the Blackfriars' Council condemned Wyclif's doctrines, the first listed was consubstantiation, the view that material bread remained in the consecrated Host while Christ also came to be present there. The list continued with the assertions that mortally sinful priests could not efficaciously administer sacraments and that the Mass's ceremonies were not divinely ordained.[3]

Later Lollards were accused of maintaining many heresies and errors, but nearly all bore some connection to Wyclif's theology. Many Lollards went dangerously beyond Wyclif's teaching of consubstantiation, and Lollards who were imprisoned and even executed were usually charged with denying that Christ was present in the Host in any form. However, their attacks against other uses of the contemporary Church—against priesthood, liturgical ceremony, confession, images, pilgrimage, and tithing—are more direct reflections of Wyclif's own views.[4] Their priesthood was, ideally, the priesthood of all the faithful, and its mission was the communication of Scripture, God's Word, through scriptural study and preaching largely unadorned by ritual.

Threatening the orthodox Church's authority and livelihood as well as its most sacred beliefs, Lollardy provoked strong countermeasures, some of which I will discuss in the pages that follow. Despite these countermeasures, however, the movement was remarkably widespread, and scholarship has consistently advanced its terminus ad quem. George Macaulay Trevelyan presents a map showing the early spread of the heresy: few parts of the south and midlands are unaffected.[5] And while historians once believed that Lollardy died out shortly after Sir John Oldcastle's unsuccessful 1414 uprising, more recent studies demonstrate continued and spreading influence well into the sixteenth century. A. G. Dickens, for example, documents considerable incidence of Lollardy in York Diocese during the period 1509–58.[6] Interestingly, however, he finds no evidence of northern Lollardy prior to this period.

In the north, then, where the Corpus Christi cycles were most concentrated, Lollardy was a belated arrival.[7] John A. F. Thomson's ground-breaking study of later Lollardy also makes it clear that the heresy was not prevalent in the area until the sixteenth century.[8] However, the movement's early failure to penetrate the north cannot be attributed to geography alone or to a lack of missionary zeal on the Lollards' part. William Thorpe, a noted

Lollard, undertook preaching tours of the north during the period 1387–1407. While his stance was not absolutely antisacramental, he did object to the doctrine of transubstantiation. He also argued that priests in a state of mortal sin could not effectively enact the sacramental ritual and that, in any case, priests' sacramental activities were far less important than their preaching of the Word. Thorpe exhorted parishioners to withhold tithes from priests who deviated from his ideal.[9] There is also evidence that Lollardy had advanced and taken hold as far north as Scotland in the early decades of the fifteenth century. According to James Edward McGoldrick, "In 1420 several heretics were seized in Scotland for preaching the English reformer's [Wyclif's] doctrines, and executions of accused Lollards took place in 1407 and 1433."[10]

Exposed to Lollardy, English northerners were slow to show its influence, and it is reasonable to question why. Perhaps orthodox clerical vigilance against Lollardy was particularly effective in the north. Of this Thomson provides some slender but suggestive evidence: "Although there do not appear to have been any cases of Lollardy in the Northern province, at least one of the officers of the church must have had an interest in it. A fifteenth-century formulary from York, which must date after 1439, contains a commission from the Archbishop to inquire about Lollards and proceed against them."[11] Thomson himself asserts, "There does not appear to be any obvious reason why the north remained almost free of heresy while it was widespread in the south."[12]

It is tempting to speculate on the nature of clerical and indeed popular vigilance against heresy in this region, for there is evidence of violent anti-Lollard sentiment among ordinary townspeople. The famous—and actually orthodox, if eccentric—holy woman, Margery Kempe of Norfolk, was passing through a Yorkshire village in 1417 when resident women ran from their houses, flailing distaffs and shouting, "Brennyth this fals heretyk."[13] Northerners were certainly more insular as well as more isolated than their southern compatriots. Culturally they were suspicious of things "sothren."[14] It is possible that the Corpus Christi plays were not only a characteristically northern expression of orthodoxy, but in fact—and perhaps intentionally—a bastion for a time against the encroaching heresy.

What evidence exists to suggest that a Corpus Christi play was a logical context and occasion for orthodox response to Lollardy? To begin, let us examine the Lollard point of view. Strikingly, although not surprisingly, the Lollards viewed the festival of

Corpus Christi with particular disdain. Included in the 1395 document, "Twelve Conclusions of the Lollards," is this assessment of the Corpus Christi liturgy (in the writing of which Saint Thomas Aquinas had a hand): "Þe seruise of Corpus Christi imad be frere Thomas is vntrewe and peyntid ful of false miraclis. And þat is no wondir, for frere Thomas þat same time, holding with þe pope, wolde haue mad a miracle of an henne ey."[15] Lollard contempt for the feast is not surprising in light of the heretics' antisacramentalism. This contempt is also evidenced in an incident that represents Lollardy's most triumphant moment at Oxford. In 1382, despite repressive efforts by the Church, the university supported the Lollard Philip Repyngdon as preacher of the Corpus Christi feast day sermon, a sermon whose orthodoxy was seriously flawed.[16]

The Lollards on this occasion co-opted a feast that the Church had instituted to celebrate the now-problematic Real Presence. Surely the Church would wish to reclaim the feast and turn its power against its detractors, and we have evidence that this happened on at least one occasion. James Gairdner recounts that Repyngdon, long recanted of his heresies by this time and now bishop of Lincoln, "felt obliged in 1419 to issue a strong admonition to the clergy of Lincoln, many of whom neglected to attend the processions long observed on Corpus Christi day and the Sunday after, in which the sacrament was solemnly borne from the church of Wigford, in the suburbs, to the cathedral."[17] Repyngdon's admonition suggests that Corpus Christi day was one on which the clergy would especially wish to present a united front. The plays performed on that day could easily have been seen as an apt vehicle for the bolstering of orthodoxy against the heretical threat.

There is further reason to explore the possibility that the plays functioned as a counter-Lollard force. Not only was there antipathy between Lollardy and the Corpus Christi feast, there was also great antipathy between Lollardy and drama per se. The Lollards' objection to religious drama was grounded in their opposition to religious images and, indeed, to all adornments of the church and of religious ceremony that, they felt, detracted from the communication of God's Word to the worshipers and embodied the danger of idolatry. Concerning images, Wyclif himself gradually moved from a moderate position to a thoroughgoing condemnation of artistic beauty, which, in his view, lacked both intrinsic virtue and power to inspire virtue in the perceiver.[18] Although Wyclif and most of his followers accepted the devotional value of the simple crucifix, even this way danger lay: "Men erren foul in þis crucifixe makyng, for þei peynten it wiþ greet cost, and hangen myche siluer and gold and precious cloþis and stones þeronne and aboute it, and suffren pore men, bouȝte wiþ Christis precious blode, to be by hem nakyd, hungry, thursty, and in strong preson boundun, þat shulden be holpyn by Cristis lawe wiþ þis ilke tresour þat is þus veynnely wastid on þes dede ymagis."[19] As W. R. Jones points out, "The Lollards were unconvinced that the average Christian made the necessary distinction between the physical object and the supernatural force it represented. . . . [They] took pride in what they characterized as the spiritual quality of their faith, which they contrasted with the alleged externalism, superficiality, and ritual conformism of orthodox religion." And of course, as Jones also suggests, the Lollard arguments against images also informed their antisacramentalism.[20] A religious drama designed to fortify veneration of the sacrament would be the very antithesis of Lollard spirituality and would be singularly abhorrent to the followers of Wyclif.

If visual adornments of the church might interfere with the practice of Christian precepts, auditory adornments could also hinder the effective communication of God's Word. Wyclif and his followers objected to the use of "fables," rhythm, and rhyme in sermons and services, as the following passages illustrate.

> certis þat prest is to blame þat shulde so frely haue þe gospel, & leeueþ þe preching þer-of & turnyþ hym to mannus fablis. for þe lawe of god dampnyþ hym þat chesiþ þe worse & þe heuyere & leeueþ þe betere & þe liȝtere, boþe to hym & to þe puple. & god axiþ not dyuysiouns ne rymes of hym þat shulde preche, but to telle euene goddis gospel & wordis to stire men þerby.[21]

> And here men shulden þenken upon to do worship to þe gospel, for it is Goddis owne word, and so worshipe God in it. Wel we witen þat a lordis word is myche chargid for his worship, and word of kyng or emperour is more chargid for his hyȝenesse. And siþ Crist is heier many weies, boþe in witt and in worship, charge his wordis for reward, siþ þis lord is greet and witti. And þis moveþ many men to hate alle oþer wordis for Cristis, and saveren hem lasse, but ȝif þei ben groundid in wordis of þe gospel. And þus men ben to blame þat docken wordis of God, and þat avoutren Goddis word, as Poul pleyneþ on many men. Þes men docken Goddis word, þat takun a word of þe gospel, and aftirward reducen þer fablis, bi rymes or oþer fals witt. And certis þis is a foul synne, for þus Goddis sentence is hid, and mannis liking is prechid; but wo worþe him þat þus doiþ![22]

Even the singing of the Mass, Wyclif suggests, can emphasize musical virtuosity—for which Wyclif appears to have had little taste—at the expense of the Word's communication. When services are "songen wiþ heiȝe criynge," music functions "to lette men fro þe sentence & vnderstondynge of þat þat was þus songen, & to maken men wery and vndisposid to studie goddis lawe for akyng of hedis."[23] Kendall pertinently associates Lollard condemnations of church music with their general objection to "ungrounded mystical experience,"[24] that is, to the de-emphasis of intellectual understanding in matters spiritual paired with the prominence of ecstatic pleasure. What the Lollards would find in the Corpus Christi plays was music itself—the shepherds' polyphonic singing in the *Secunda Pastorum*, for example—along with a great many other stimuli to aesthetic response.

Without any evidence beyond this—Lollard condemnation of images, fables, rhyme, and song—we should have no difficulty in understanding why the Lollards would strenuously object to the Corpus Christi plays, in which God's Word was embroidered upon in all these ways. We also know that Wyclif was suspicious of the guilds, the plays' frequent producers, as fraternities—like the monastic orders—whose existence conflicted with the Christian ideal of universal brotherhood.[25] And some distrust of religious plays themselves is evident in writings attributed by nineteenth-century scholars to Wyclif. Wyclif would have it both ways, in that he is perfectly willing to cite the York Paternoster play as evidence for the acceptability of translated Scripture,[26] but elsewhere he complains of those who "loken to veyn plaies"[27] and—less ambiguously—of attention given not to the best preachers but instead to him "þat kan best pleie a pagyn of þe deuyl."[28] Later Lollards were less equivocal and more vociferous in their view of religious drama: two important sources merit examination. One of these is a Lollard poem of the late fourteenth or early fifteenth century attacking drama performed by friars:

> Went I forther on my way in that same tyde,
> Ther I sawe a frere blede in myddes of his syde,
> Bothe in hondes and in fete had he woundes wyde.[29]

Although friars did not act in the Corpus Christi cycles, this poem is significant in documenting Lollard opposition to, especially, the staging of the Passion. Its tone suggests that the author is not merely mocking "crude" theater,[30] but that he finds such theater blasphemous: "Thai haue mo goddes than we," asserts the Lollard poet, speaking of friar-actors who dare to portray Christ himself.[31]

Our second source is the much-cited *Tretise of Miraclis Pleyinge*, a late fourteenth-century Lollard document.[32] Here the author's references to dramatic depictions of Christ's Passion— but not exclusively to clerical actors—make it probable that the Corpus Christi plays themselves were among his targets. He finds the plays blasphemous and conducive not to piety, but to immoral revelry and idolatry. And, not unexpectedly, we find here again the argument the Lollards used against images and rhyming sermon material.

> Sithen no man may serven two lordis togydere, as seith Crist in his gospel, no man may heren at onys efectuely the voice of oure maister Crist and of his owne lustis. And sithen miraclis pleyinge is of the lustis of the fleyssh and mirthe of the body, no man may efectuely heeren hem and the voice of Crist at onys, as the voice of Crist and the voice of the fleysh ben of two contrarious lordis.[33]

Religious drama is an idolatrous distraction, and its viewers inevitably undervalue or ignore God's Word. Just as the children of Israel, in Moses' absence, made and worshiped idols,

> so unkindely seyen men nowe on days, "Crist doth now no miraclis for us, pleye we therfore his olde," adding many lesingis therto so colowrably that the puple gife as myche credense to hem as to the trwthe. And so they forgeten to ben percener of the prayere of Crist, for the maumetrye that men don to siche miraclis pleyinge— maumetrie, I seye, for siche pleyinge men as myche honoryn (or more than) the word of God whanne it is prechid, and therfore blasfemely thei seyen that siche pleyinge doith more good than the word of God whanne it is prechid to the puple.[34]

Lollards themselves, then, saw religious drama as embodying much of what they most objected to in the orthodox Church. But did the Church in late medieval England see religious drama similarly, that is, as a powerful embodiment of its most exalted— and most embattled—tenets? To approach this question, I will begin with an overview of the ways in which the Church did exert its power against heresy. Cecilia Cutts suggests that, in countering Lollardy, the Church's methods were "of two types: (1) those intended to frighten and coerce people into orthodoxy; (2) those which aimed to instruct and persuade."[35] We are not here concerned with methods in the former category such as the statute *De haeretico comburendo* (1401), which provided for the execution, by burning, of convicted heretics. The latter category, however, includes the licensing and commissioning of special preachers and polemical writers and, according to Cutts, "possibly also . . . the presentation of religious plays."[36]

The prevalent orthodox attitude toward drama stands in sharp contrast to the Lollards'. To begin, the very basic iconoclasm at the center of Lollard antipathy to drama was not in the mainstream of contemporary orthodoxy (although, as I have discussed in the Introduction, the Lollards were hardly the first Christians to oppose the use of images). On the contrary, as Peter Travis points out, such writers as Thomas Netter (d. 1430)—the learned Carmelite and "hammer of the Lollards"—argued "that Christ gave his blessing to images by the very act of his own Incarnation." Travis continues, "Just as it was Christ in carnal form who reformed fallen man, so it was the carnality of the artistic image, its power of appealing to the five senses, that was held by apologists to be its special educative strength."[37] To be sure, plays were not quite the same as static images, and some orthodox clergymen voiced suspicions of religious drama, particularly when priests were the actors.[38] On the other hand, as G. R. Owst illustrates, there was widespread belief among the contemporary orthodox clergy that religious drama could be performed for virtuous reasons and to good effect: "Following the good example of William Melton and the unknown author of *Dives et Pauper*, rejecting the disdain of Robert Mannyng and John Bromyard, they would approve with *Pauper* of 'miracles, pleyes and daunces' done mainly for devotion, honesty and mirth, without ribaldry, taint of heresy, or indecency, and without keeping men from divine service or 'fro goddes worde hering.' "[39]

To this moderate approbation of religious drama, we can add evidence of more ardent enthusiasm. The above-mentioned William Melton, a Minorite friar, is reported to have preached in favor of the York Corpus Christi pageants in 1426, recommending "the aforesaid play to the people; affirming that it was good in it self and very commendable so to do."[40] Still more to the point is the virtual certainty that the Corpus Christi plays are products of clerical authorship: the theological sophistication evident in the plays has been identified by many scholars as a voice of the orthodox Church. So there were certainly members of the clergy in the fourteenth and fifteenth centuries who were invested in the religious, educative use of the stage.

And why was such education needed? David Mills suggests

that religious drama "arises from the need to explain the [religious] ritual and hence presupposes a 'non-believer' who readily becomes a hostile sceptic. In affirming, the plays also defend and in defending they attest hostility."[41] Although it is not demonstrable that all the cycles were produced by guilds—and the evidence for Towneley is especially slight—it is worth noting that the selective solidarity of the guilds (a target, as I have noted, of Wyclif's censure) may also bear witness to such hostility. In addition to the many economic and social reasons for guild membership, such organizations might have served as a collective mode of announcing and protecting one's orthodoxy.[42]

More important, the Corpus Christi celebration itself could have served as such a communal announcement, drawing diverse individuals, groups, and classes together into the unified "body" of which they were part and distinguishing that entity from the outsider. In an important article that speaks to the significance both of the plays and of their corporate production, Mervyn James discusses the "social dimension" of the cult of Corpus Christi, its role in strengthening the social order against dissension and fragmentation. He argues

> that the theme of Corpus Christi is society seen in terms of body; and that the concept of body provided urban societies with a mythology and ritual in terms of which the opposites of social wholeness and social differentiation could be both affirmed, and also brought into a creative tension, one with the other. The final intention of the cult was, then, to express the social bond and to contribute to social integration. . . . The mass . . . both affirmed and created the symbol of social body, which was the Body of Christ. The Corpus Christi procession involved the application of this theme to a specific community and place, presenting in visual form the structure of social differentiation taken up into the social wholeness which was the town itself.[43]

Thus, the Corpus Christi celebration, including the contribution of cycle pageants by various groups (be they guilds or other social units), represented and enhanced the "wholeness" of the community. As a communal celebration, it attested to the town's piety and therefore implicitly to its solidarity against definitionally external heretical forces. It also might have served to beat the Lollards at their own game. Many a Lollard preacher would identify and attempt to capitalize on social dissatisfactions, urging that only a break from the social and clerical establishment could bring people to a better, more spiritualized life. The Corpus Christi celebrations, especially the plays themselves, "provided a mechanism . . . whereby the tensions implicit in the diachronic rise and fall of occupational communities could be confronted and worked out."[44] Corpus Christi created a social body that was a *concordia discors* and highly proof against antisocial doctrine.

Might it not have occurred to the Corpus Christi playwrights, writing in many cases for guild producers and actors, not only to bolster orthodoxy, but specifically to counter heresy? We cannot definitively answer this question; however, in the case of two later fifteenth-century noncycle plays, we may be reasonably certain that this purpose underlies some part of their design. The best known and most beautifully crafted of the English morality plays, *Everyman* (ca. 1495), contains what has been called a "digression" on the priesthood. Digression it may be in its arresting of the play's central action, but not in terms of the playwright's overall purpose. This dramatist is interested not only in communicating orthodox doctrine concerning repentance, but also in making certain that his audience will be able to avoid particular heretical pitfalls. Everyman's restoration to grace requires that he confess to a priest from whom he receives absolution and the sacrament. Lollards, as we have seen, questioned the efficacy of priesthood as well as the nature of the sacrament. In this context it is significant that Everyman's Five Wittes comments specifically on priests:

> God hath to them more power given
> Than to ony aungell that is in heven.
> With five wordes he may consecrate
> Goddes body in flesshe and blode to make,
> And handeleth his Maker bitwene his hande[s].
>
> (735–39)[45]

The play admits of criticism of "sinfull preestes" (759), but no suggestion is made that, as the Lollards would have it, such priests cannot efficaciously make the sacrament. Further, Five Wittes can barely credit the existence of sinful clergymen: "I trust to God no suche may we finde, / Therfore let us Preesthode honour" (764–65).

Counter-Lollardy is still more pronounced and, indeed, programmatic in another later fifteenth-century play, the Croxton *Play of the Sacrament.*[46] This play—in contrast to many plays so termed—is literally a "miracle play." It depicts a Eucharistic miracle in which a consecrated Host, variously mistreated by a group of Jews, first bleeds and then transforms itself into an image of Christ "with woundys bledying" (s.d. following 712). Spectacularly as such a miracle could be staged, this play's content is determined more by doctrinal than by dramatic considerations. The play's teaching, as Cutts points out, includes "not only transubstantiation, but also baptism, confession, penance, pilgrimage, respect for images, reverence for the Blessed Virgin, the spiritual power and authority of a priest and the reverence due him, and the superior power and authority of a Bishop, which is notably greater than that of a priest."[47] As Cutts convincingly demonstrates, these tenets have a common denominator: all are points of orthodox doctrine challenged or denied by the Lollards. The Croxton play was designed to function as counter-Lollard propaganda.

One point d'appui for Cutts's argument that she does not employ is an anti-Lollard pun which appears in the play. Toward the end of the drama, the abusers of the Host, now newly converted, verbally repent of their heresy, their doubt of Christ's Real Presence in the sacrament. Ser Jonathas the Jew says, "Now wyll we walke by contré and cost, / Owr wyckyd lyuyng for to restore" (965). Arystorius, his accomplice, likewise promises "to amende myn wyckyd lyfe" (973). The repetition—"wyckyd lyuyng" and "wyckyd lyfe"—is hardly coincidental. Repenting of their wicked—that is, heretical—behavior, the play's characters employ wordplay that defines their heresy precisely. To repent of "wyckyd lyfe" is to repent of being a Wycliffite, a Lollard. This pun, used consciously as part of the play's counter-Lollardy, did not originate with the Croxton playwright. Thomas Netter makes use of a Latin version of the pun in his *Doctrinale Fidei Ecclesiae Catholicae contra Wicklevistas et Hussitas*. In this polemic, commissioned by Henry V and written in the 1420s, Netter refers to the heresiarch as "Joanne, cognomento impiae vitae": "John Wicked-Life."[48]

The religious drama, then, was not only potentially an effective weapon against heresy; it actually functioned as such in at least these two plays. In the case of the Corpus Christi drama it is likely that some of the plays the cycles comprise originally antedated Wyclif's life. However, the first references to full cycle performances about which we can be certain point to the year 1378;[49] significantly, Wyclif first began openly to doubt Eucharistic orthodoxy in the early seventies, and in 1377 he was first imprisoned. It was also around 1377 that Wyclif's ideas began to be disseminated by "Poor Priests" traveling throughout the country.[50] Hence in 1378 there was ample cause, from the Church's perspective, for a bolstering of orthodox beliefs against the taint of specific heresies. The emerging cycle tradition embodied a power that surely could function in just this way.

2

The Major Controversies: Theologies of the Word and the Sacrament

To explore the possibility of counter-Lollard content in the Towneley plays, it is necessary to analyze closely two major areas of controversy between the heretics and the orthodox Church. The first of these was Eucharistic theology. While Wyclif's belief in consubstantiation did not involve a denial of Christ's Real Presence in the Host, the theologian's Scholastic equivocations concerning the nature of that Presence left his followers room for a wide range of interpretations. In a sermon for the Feast of Corpus Christi, for example, Wyclif expresses his doctrine thus:

> Þes ben to rude heretikes, þat seien þei eten Crist bodili, and seien þei parten ech membre of him,—nekke, bac, heed, and foot. And alle siche heresies springen, for þei witen not what þis oost is. Þis oost is breed in his kynde, as ben oþer oostes unsacrid, and sacramentaliche Goddis bodi; for Crist seiþ so, þat mai not lye.[1]

"Sacramentaliche" remains disturbingly undefined. Similarly, the "Prima confessio Wyclyf de sacramento" creates ambiguities in its opening sentences:

> I knowleche þat þe sacrament of þe auter is verrey Goddus body in fourme of brede, but it is in anoþer maner Godus body þan it is in heuene. For in heuen it is seue fote in fourme and figure of flesshe and blode. But in þe sacrament Goddus body is be myracle of God in fourme of brede, and he is nouþer of seuen fote, ne in mannes figure.[2]

Wyclif saw in the doctrine of transubstantiation the dangerous grounding for such idolatry as also characterized the veneration of saints' relics. The orthodox emphasis on the supernatural and the suspension of the ordinary laws of the universe resulted in a

Eucharistic devotion that was, if aweful, also external and super-
stitious—not an interior experience of communion with God.[3]

Wyclif's followers, many of whom lacked his intellectual sophistication, often distorted his argument. If the bread the worshiper could see was really there, then it was difficult to accept
that Christ was also really there. Perhaps he was "sacramentally"
or "spiritually" present, but such a presence was much less
compelling to the worshiper than the Real Presence of orthodox
doctrine. Some Lollards, denying the presence altogether, asserted that any veneration of the sacramental elements amounted
to idolatry: "Þe feynid miracle of þe sacrament of bred inducith
alle men but a fewe to ydolatrie, for þei wene þat Godis bodi, þat
neuere schal out of heuene, be uertu of þe prestis wordis schulde
ben closid essenciali in a litil bred þat þei schewe to þe puple."[4]
Wyclif himself argued that the Mass had no scriptural foundation: the sixth heresy found by the Blackfriars' Council was
"Quod pertinaciter asserere non est fundatum in Evangelio quod
Christus missam ordinaverit."[5] While such an assertion indeed
robbed the Mass of some of its dignity and authority, Wyclif
never denied that its sacramental core was sacrificial.[6] Nonetheless, those many Lollards who denied the Real Presence viewed
the Mass as lacking not only in scriptural warrant but also in
sacrificial, redemptive efficacy.

The sacrament's sacrificial efficacy was central to orthodox
belief. Since the twelfth century, the Church had maintained the
doctrine of transubstantiation: at the moment of consecration,
Christ became present in the sacramental elements, and the
material bread and wine were no longer present. By virtue of this
Real Presence, the Mass's sacrificial action became an actual
enactment of the eternally present sacrifice on Calvary. Thus, the
sacrament of the Mass became the sole channel by which the
redemptive power of Christ's sacrifice reached the worshiper.
This sacrificial focus is clear in a late fourteenth-century orthodox sermon addressed to parishioners who might have been
endangered by Lollard teachings.

> And ryght þe same body þat died on þe Crosse and þis day rose verry
> God and man, þe same bodie is on þe Sacrament on þe awtur in forme
> of brede. Þus bereþ he wittenesse in þe gospell Iohanis, þer he seis
> þus, "Ego sum panis viuus, qui de celo descendi. Si quis man-
> ducauerit ex hoc pane, viuet in eternum—I am," seiþ Crist, "þe brede
> of liff, þat commeþ from heuen. And who-so etis here-of, he shall live
> withowten ende."[7]

The Real Presence is the agent of salvation, the homilist avers. To deny its existence is to become nonparticipant in the redemptive sacrifice. Another noteworthy contemporary sermon appears in the late fourteenth-century collection known as *Mirk's Festial*.[8] This is a Corpus Christi sermon that places strong emphasis on the Passion, thereby connecting the Eucharist with Christ's redemptive suffering and death. Interestingly, Alan J. Fletcher theorizes that the *Festial* may have been designed to counter Lollardy.

> There may be nothing quite so effective as the scent of heresy to precipitate the orthodox establishment into motion, and perhaps we should suggest . . . that he [Mirk] was also conscious of a need to help arm the Church against what he saw as a spiritual threat. . . . At the very least, the *Festial* should be regarded as the product of the same decade as saw the public condemnation of Wycliffe and the growing unease of the orthodox establishment with the content and implications of Wycliffite thought.[9]

As Fletcher suspects counter-Lollard intent in Mirk's sermon cycle, so it is reasonable to raise the issue of counter-Lollardy in a cycle of plays embodying, as I shall demonstrate, similar theological emphases.

The second of the two major areas of controversy between orthodoxy and Lollard heresy can be defined in terms of the theology of God's Word. The Church claimed, for its priests, the power of consecration and, for its central ritual, the power of redemption. Lollardy denied the validity of both claims, but the movement was by no means exclusively one of negation. The Lollards presented a clear alternative program to those whom they would convert. The priesthood, now at best misguided, at worst corrupt, could potentially redeem itself. By turning from ritual toward simple but fervent preaching, the clergy could fulfill their mission to disseminate God's Word to the people. But the clergy must not then monopolize the Word as they had monopolized the rituals. The laity, Lollards believed strongly, must have access to the Bible in English that they might actively pursue the study of the Word and thereby seek salvation through their own hard, studious efforts.

As Kendall puts it, the vision at the center of Lollardy was of "a new kind of church . . . centered on the hearth rather than the altar and ritually united through the spiritual consumption of his word rather than his body. . . . [F]or the Lollard the study of the

Bible was a ritual activity, an act of devotion in which the Real
Presence might be as or more authentically perceived than in the
Eucharist itself."[10] In other words, while the Church stressed the
sacraments and—to some degree—de-emphasized preaching,
Wyclif's view was the reverse. As Trevelyan asserts, "It was his
avowed object to make people attach more importance to the
pulpit than to the Sacraments."[11] Herbert B. Workman draws
from several of Wyclif's writings to express concisely the reformer's view: "'Mute prelates', whom he compares to 'dumb
idols' or 'waterless clouds', were 'the ruin of the Church', for
'evangelical preaching' alone could stop the growth of sin, and is
'more precious than the administration of any sacrament'. By
preaching, Christ effected more than by all His miracles."[12]
Wycklyffes Wycket stresses the Lollard view that the Mass was
not divinely ordained, arguing instead for the preeminence of the
Word.

> He [Christ] toke bread and blessed, & yet what blessed he. The
> Scripture saythe not that Christ toke bread and blessed it, or that he
> blessed the breade whiche he had taken.
>   Therfore it semeth more that he blessed his dysciples and apostels,
> whom he hade ordayned witnesses of his passion, and in them he
> lefte his blessed worde whiche is the bread of lyfe, as it is wrytten not
> onlye in brede lyued man, but in euery worde that procedith out of
> the mouthe of God. Also Christe saith, I am the breade of lyfe that
> came downe from heuen, and Christe saith often in Mathew, the
> wordes that I haue spoken to you be spirite and lyfe.[13]

Lollard preachers took their mandate seriously. William
Thorpe, for example, "described his shock and annoyance, as he
was preaching in St. Chad's Shrewsbury, on Sunday 17 April
1407, when his audience suddenly deserted him at the sound of
the sacring bell. Thorpe chided them. Seeing the sacrament was
of far less value than hearing the word of God."[14] Margaret Aston
discusses the Lollards' belief in the sacramental value of the
Word: "'For the Word is God and God is the Word', as John
Whitehorne put it in 1499. 'And therefore whosoever receive
devoutly God's Word he receiveth the very body of Christ.'"[15]
Workman further clarifies Wyclif's stress on preaching and the
spiritual centrality of God's Word as opposed to sacramental rite.

> In Wyclif's judgement lack of preaching based upon the Word alone
> was the cause of the spiritual deadness of the age; it was as if one
> were to prepare a meal without bread. God's Word, especially the
> Gospels, is the seed which brings regeneration and spiritual life. . . .

There is one point in particular to which Wyclif draws attention—Christian men who preach the Gospel must give the first place to Gospel history, for in that history is grounded the faith of the Church.

According to Wyclif, God's Word is embodied in the Bible: Scripture has supreme authority, and all other writings, Church teachings, and rituals are at best secondary.[16]
Wyclif's reverence for the "pure" Word and his near contempt for extrabiblical Church documents reverberate through his homiletic writings.

> Luk seiþ þat he is blessid þat heeriþ and keepiþ Goddis word; and siþ a lordis word is worshiped after þe gretnesse of þis lord, and Crist is more wiþouten mesure þan ony kyng or erþeli lord, how loveþ þe peple Crist, but after þat it loveþ Cristis word? And þis bileve seiþ Poul, ʒif man love not Jesus Crist, he is cursid of God, and þat is more þan mannis curse. Cursid be he þat wolde ordeyne þat þe pistilis and þe gospelis weren turned in to decrees or decretalis of þe Pope. For as no word of Goddis lawe haþ ony strengþe, but as Crist spekiþ it, so no word of mannis lawe shulde be loved but if Crist speke it.[17]

Following Wyclif, not only do Lollards oppose the validity of nonscriptural decrees and decretals, but they also object to certain forms of exegesis, which they view as false addition to the Word.

> What power han þan worldly prelatis to make so many wickid lawes? siþ god curseþ hem þat maken wickid lawes, & comaundiþ þat no man schal adde to his wordis ne draw fro hem vp peyne of grete cursynge of god & dampnynge in helle. Þat is to seie þat no man adde false sentence ne false glose to holy writt, for þan, as ierom seiþ, he is an heretik; and þat no man drawe ony treuþe fro goddis wordis, for þei enclosen alle nedeful treuþe & profitable for mannys soule. & to þis entente siþ poul in his pistel þat ʒif ony man, ʒee apostil or angel of heuene, preche oþer þing þan is tauʒte of crist & his apostelis he is cursid. And Seint Jon seiþe, in þe ende of þe apocalips, þat ʒif ony man adde þus to goddis wordis, god schal brynge vpon hym alle þe vengaunces wryten in þe apocalips, & ʒif any man wiþdrawe þus fro goddis wordis god schall don hym out of þe bok of lif.[18]

To be sure, Lollards did produce glosses and commentaries of their own, especially in the early period, when Lollardy was still largely the province of university men. These writings are quite conventional in their copious citation of patristic authority. As Anne Hudson asserts, they "were evidently inspired by a desire to make available in the vernacular a bulk of traditional exegesis of a kind that would facilitate the understanding of the literal sense at the centre of the biblical message." But Lollards objected vehemently to such "glosing" as they perceived to stem from "modern sophistication" and to distort the biblical message or add to it, turning Scripture into "fable."[19] Any ornamentation of the Word, even for educative purposes, was pernicious.

Orthodoxy, of course, did not diverge in principle from the Lollards' veneration of the Word: the dissemination of God's Word had been the Church's program since the time of the Gospels. Where the factions differed was in precisely what God's Word comprised—and therefore how it might best be disseminated. Most importantly, the Wycliffite insistence on the literal, unexplicated meaning of Scripture was anathema to the orthodox churchman, who invoked the dictum, "the letter killeth."[20] The letter killed, indeed, because it was only partial truth—a little knowledge, and very dangerous. Thomas Netter focused his anti-Lollard *Doctrinale Fidei* on Wyclif's misperception of the Word. In the work's prologue, as James Gairdner points out,

> first of all he expresses his abhorrence that Wycliffe, in all his arguments, should cut the Christian faith in two, and only accept the one-half; for Wycliffe, he says, pretends that he admits the faith of the Scriptures, but he neglects that faith of the whole Christian Church which Jesus Christ, and even St. Paul, delivered unwritten, and without which any one errs, no matter how much of the Scriptures he brings forward.[21]

God's Word—his Law—in the orthodox view quite definitely embodied nonscriptural material, as this fourteenth-century homilist declares:

> We must also beleue þat euery parte principall of Goddes lawe aftur þe vndirstondyng of þe Holygoost is feyȝthfull and trew, y-ordeynd for mans saluacion: quia "Lex Domini inmaculata, conuertens animas," in Psalmo. And farþur we must beleue þat þoo þinges þat ben in þe mater of feyȝthe determyned by Cristes churche ben trewe, and suche determynacions and ordinaunce, to obeye þem, for it is Cristes commaundement, þe wiche seyþ to is apostels and to oþur prelates by hem, "Qui vos audit, me audit; et qui vos spernit, me spernit," Luce xⁿ.[22]

Another contemporary orthodox sermon appears to address Lollard objections on this issue. The homilist, exhorting his listeners on the importance of understanding God's law, imagines the dilemma of a parishioner who has come into contact with Lollardy. The preacher is aware that some Lollards overstate the Church's possessiveness concerning the Word of God: " 'Sir,' þou seiste, parauntur, 'it is forbede by ȝou prestes and prelates of holychurche anny lewde man to entermette of holywritte.' Sir, I sey naye: but itt is forbede anny lewde man to mysvse holywritt, for God hym-selfe biddeþ is peple to vndirstonde itt." But, the preacher continues, that which the laity need to understand of God's law—the Pater Noster, the Ave Maria, the Creed, the Deca- logue, and selected other tenets—is precisely what they would learn from listening to the many orthodox sermons preached about these articles. Indeed, contrary to Lollard claims, many sermons were preached by the more attentive parish clergy. The laity, since "all mowe not com to þe perfite vndirstondynge þer-of for sotelte of þis lawe and oþur werldely occupacions,"[23] require the assistance of the priesthood—not an Englished Bible—to gain access to God's Word.

The laity would gain access to the Word not only through the preaching they heard in church, but also through the Mass ritual as a whole. According to the orthodox *Lay-Folks Mass-Book*, the priest beginning Mass takes on the awesome task of conveying God's Word. The priest "has mikel nede of grace":

> for þen an erthly mon shal neuen
> þo wordes of ihesu crist, gods son of heuen,
> bothe þo reders & þo herers
> has mykil nede, me þenk, of lerers,
> how þai shulde rede, & þai shulde here
> þo wordes of god, so leue & dere
> Men aght to haue ful mikel drede,
> when þai shuld here or els hit rede.

The author instructs the worshipers to begin their devotions by crossing themselves and praying to the Trinity: "Bi gods worde welcome to me."[24]

When the writer comes to his discussion of the Gospel section of the Mass, he not surprisingly seeks to reinforce his audience's awe and reverence for the Word. In sharp contrast to the Lollard emphasis on hard study and reasoned understanding, the ortho- dox spokesman delineates a more mystical notion of the receiv- ing of God's Word, a receiving that need not be mediated by intellect or understanding.

þauӡ ӡe vnderstonde • hit nouӡt,
Ӡe may wel wite • þat god hit wrouӡt,
And þerfore • wisdam were hit
For to worschupe • al godes werkes
To lewed men • þat ben none clerkes:
þis lesson • now go lere hit.[25]

These lines are followed by an exemplum describing how an adder may be charmed despite its not understanding the language used in the spell, and the author draws a parallel between the adder and the unscholarly worshiper:

So fareþ • þer vnderstondyng fayles,
þe verrey vertu • ӡow alle a-vayles
þorw grace • þat god ӡow grauntes.[26]

As the tract's editor suggests, this not altogether felicitous exemplum may have been added after the Lollards began their campaign for vernacular Scriptures.[27] To be sure, orthodoxy also involved apprehension of specific scriptural content, but this appealing notion of an effortless mystical reception of the Word assumes centrality in the battle against Lollardy.

Finally, at the close of the Mass, the worshiper is urged to pay special attention to another passage of inaccessible, yet efficacious Latin.

. . . forӡete not • þe god-spelle
    For þing • þat may bi-falle.
Tac a good entent • þer-to
Hit is • þe Inprincipio
    On latin • þat men calle,
a ӡer and fourti dayes • atte lest
For verbum caro factum est
    To pardoun • haue ӡe schalle.[28]

While the reading of the prologue of John's Gospel was a late addition to the Mass, it was considered a potent one. As Joseph A. Jungmann asserts, these verses about the Word's Incarnation were "rightly regarded as a summary of the Gospel, the divine power of which is, in a measure, concentrated there."[29] Here is further evidence of orthodoxy's view that God's Word was embodied in and transmitted through the Mass.

Still more importantly, the Church could claim, countering Lollardy, that it was providing the laity with God's Word in a yet

more powerful form, the most powerful form available in the Age
of Grace. While the Lollards saw the Word as itself sacramental,
orthodoxy made the same equation in reverse. There was no need
for intensified preaching efforts or for an Englished Bible, for
God's Word was embodied in the Eucharistic sacrament. The
Word—made flesh—was identical with the sacramental Presence. In physical or spiritual communion, the worshiper could
quite literally take in the Word. By viewing Word and sacrament
as one, orthodoxy provided a simple but elegant counter to both
of Lollardy's chief criticisms: the Church's comparative de-emphasis of preaching and its stress on ritual.

The Church did indeed view Word and sacrament as one, and
the equation had a long history. The identification of Christ as the
Word Incarnate, of course, originally derives from the prologue to
the Gospel according to John: "And the Word became flesh and
dwelt among us, full of grace and truth" (John 1:14). Among
theologians of the first centuries, the identification was extended
to apply to the sacrament of Christ's Presence. Origen (185?–
254?) refers to the Eucharist as the flesh and blood of the Word of
God.[30] Athanasius (ca. 297–373) describes the consecration in
terms of the Word's descent into the bread and the chalice.[31]
Saint Jerome explicitly associates the sacrament with the Word of
Holy Scripture.

> Legimus sanctas scripturas. Ego corpus Iesu euangelium puto; sanc-
> tas scripturas puto doctrinam eius. Et quando dicit *Qui non com-*
> *ederit carnem meam et biberit sanguinem meum,* licet in mysterio
> possit intellegi, tamen uere . . . corpus Christi et sanguis eius sermo
> scriptuarum est, doctrina diuina est. [We read holy Scripture. I be-
> lieve the body of Jesus to be the gospel; I believe holy Scripture to be
> his doctrine. And when he says, *He who will not eat my body and*
> *drink my blood,* I understand this to be true mystically . . . the body
> of Christ and his blood are the Word of Scripture, it is divine doc-
> trine.][32]

Jerome's words, curiously enough, could be taken to uphold the
Lollard theology of the Word, were it not for the fact that the
sacrament's essentiality forms part of the subtext. What emerges,
indeed, from patristic dicta is the sense of a continuous "history"
of the Word culminating, from the earthly human perspective, in
its sacramental manifestation.

It is not only in patristic theology that the Word-sacrament
identity is manifested. While the medieval period saw shifts in
definition of the sacraments' meaning and relative importance,

the understanding of the Eucharist retained its connection with the theology of the Word. In the ninth century, Eucharistic controversy raged between Paschasius Radbertus and Ratramnus of Corbie. The theologians differed on the issue of transubstantiation, the nature and occurrence of substantial change in the elements; but both defined the sacrament as the Word of God. Paschasius says of the Eucharist that "caro verbi fit esca in hoc mysterio [the flesh of the Word is eaten in this mystery]."[33] Similarly, Ratramnus describes the invisible existence in the sacrament of "verbum Dei, qui est panis vivus [the Word of God, who is the living bread]."[34]

The theology of the Word was itself developed and systematized most fully in the *Summa Theologiae* of Saint Thomas Aquinas, which is characterized by its organization and consideration of all things in terms of their relation to the Word. As M.-D. Chenu states, "Each one of its elements, by its location within theology, is referred, from within, to God and to the word of God."[35] According to Thomas, "The causal plan of all God's works is contained in the Word";[36] and the Thomist understanding of sacramentality fully reflects this axiom. In the prologue to his analysis of the sacraments, Thomas says, "POST CONSIDERATIONEM eorum quae pertinent ad mysteria Verbi incarnati, considerandum est de Ecclesiae sacramentis, quae ab ipso Verbo incarnato efficaciam habent [Now that we have completed our consideration of the mysteries of the Incarnate Word, our next field of investigation is the sacraments of the Church, seeing that it is from this same Incarnate Word that these derive their efficacy]."[37] The Incarnate Word is the "sanctifying cause"[38] of the sacraments. David Bourke concisely expresses the Thomist view: "A sacrament is the sign of the incarnate Word, his Passion and Resurrection, as sanctifying man, a sign which actually causes what it signifies by an efficient causality flowing from God through the humanity of Christ and present intrinsically in the sign itself."[39] This understanding permeates both the theological and the devotional writings of Thomas; the hymns he composed for the Feast of Corpus Christi focus strikingly on the divine Word. The hymn *Pange lingua*, composed for matins of the feast day, stresses the Word's operation in the sacramental miracle.[40] Another hymn, beginning "Verbum supernum prodiens," celebrates the Eucharist by describing the progression of the Word from the Father, Christ's institution of the sacrament, his death, and his return to glory: the "history" of the Word and its sacramental culmination.[41]

Thomas also played a role in the selection and arrangement of readings for the Corpus Christi liturgy. Jerome Taylor, in his analysis of the feast's liturgy, argues that these texts provide "a conspectus of God's works through numerous allusions which relate these works to the Eucharist."[42] Taylor believes that the message the liturgy conveys is that the Eucharist is to be celebrated as a "comprehensive commemoration of all God's wonders."[43] It is not the comparatively static commemorative function of the Eucharist, however, but the common denominator among the sacrament and God's other "marvels" that the Corpus Christi readings most forcefully assert. For example, Taylor cites one of the readings for the feast's octave as revealing the association between God's work of Creation and its Eucharistic commemoration.

> "How is it that what is bread, is the body of Christ?" asks Ambrose. He answers: by the word of Christ, by the word of him of whom it is written, "The Lord commanded, and the heaven was made; the Lord commanded, and the earth was made; . . . the Lord commanded, and every creature was brought forth. . . . 'He spoke and they were made; he commanded, and they were created.' And so I say to you, before consecration this was not the body of Christ; but after consecration it is the body of Christ. For he spoke and it became so; he himself commanded, and it was created so."[44]

The point of this passage is not primarily to remind us of one of God's great works in a Eucharistic context; rather, it is to exhort belief in the Real Presence, explaining the miracle of transubstantiation by attributing it to the omnipotent Word's operative presence: the words of consecration are identical in nature with the Word of Creation. This emphasis is strikingly reflected at various other points throughout the Corpus Christi liturgy. In another of the octave's matins' readings, several miracles are recounted, and this conclusion is drawn:

> Quod si tantum valuit humana benedictio ut naturam converteret, quid dicemus de ipsa consecratione divine, ubi ipsa verba Domini ac Salvatoris operantur? Nam sacramentum istud quod accepimus sermone Christi conficitur. Quod si tantum valuit sermo Helyae ut ignem de caelo deponeret: nonne valebit Christi sermo ut species mutet elementorum? [And if a human blessing was so powerful as to change nature, what shall we say of this divine consecration, wherein operates the Word of the Lord and Savior? For we receive the sacrament that Christ's Word makes. And if Elijah's word was so powerful as to call down fire from the sky, is not Christ's Word powerful enough to change the form of elements?][45]

In another reading the words of consecration are discussed as follows:

> Antequam consecratur panis est: ubi autem verba Christi ac-cesserunt, Corpus Christi est. Deinde audi dicentum: Accipite, et edite ex hoc omnes, hoc est corpus meum. Et ante verba Christi calix est vino et aqua plenus; ubi autem verba Christi operata fuerint, ibi sanguis efficitur qui plebum redemit. Vide ergo quam potens est sermo Christi universa convertere. [Before consecration it is bread: however, when Christ's words are added, it is the body of Christ. Then listen to the words: Take, all, and eat of this, this is my body. And before Christ's words, the chalice is full of wine and water; however, when Christ's words shall have operated, there is made the blood that redeems the people. Therefore see how powerful is the Word of Christ to change the universe.][46]

Thus, the Eucharist is set forth as a manifestation of the divine Word. Other miracles are adduced not so much because they are commemorated in the sacrament, as because they too reveal the presence and function of that Word. A recurrent message of the Corpus Christi liturgy is encapsulized in the final sentence quoted above: *Therefore see how powerful is the Word of Christ to change the universe.* Orthodox theology of the Word exhorts belief in the Word's omnipotence, demonstrates the continuum of the Word in history, and stresses its culminating sacramental embodiment.

* * *

To possess a deeply engrained sensitivity to the Word, its nature, its power, and its progression to sacramental fulfillment, the medieval Christian need not have been familiar with patristic or Scholastic writings. The rhythm of this fulfillment permeated medieval life, informing the design of the liturgical year. The movement from Septuagesima, with its Old Testament readings beginning at Gen. 1:1, to Easter Sunday provided the churchgoer with an overview of the multiple forms of God's Word and its progression.[47] And just as the year progressed to its emotional and sacramental climax on Easter Sunday—the day on which most layfolk experienced their single annual sacramental communion—so the Mass progressed through the service of readings to its climax of consecration and communion. As Jungmann puts it:

> The reading of Holy Scripture represents the proper content of the fore-Mass in much the same way as the Sacrament forms the heart of

the Mass proper; they are both precious treasures which the Church safeguards for mankind. Just as our Lord himself first taught, and only after this foundation was laid did He erect his kingdom, so now too the word of God should first fill our soul before the mystery of the New Covenant is realized among us anew.[48]

At Mass, the worshiper would apprehend the Word's progression from scriptural teaching to sacramental mystery. This sense of progression would have been heightened still further by visual means: the "Epistle side" and the "Gospel side" of the altar. For the first of the Mass's two readings, the priest stood on the south side of the sanctuary. Although this reading is called the "Epistle," it does not always come from the Apostles' letters; indeed, it is sometimes taken from the Old Testament. The priest's movements would visually have suggested a progression of the Word when he moved from the south to the north side of the altar to read the Gospel. This suggestion would have been intensified by the contrast between what Jungmann terms the "sobriety" of the Epistle reading and the heightened ceremonial of the Gospel.[49] Climactically, the ceremonial of the Canon of the Mass was still more impressive. Like the movement from Septuagesima to Easter Sunday, the movement from Introit to Communion was a familiar manifestation of the action whereby the Word, once spoken by God and his prophets, then incarnated, at last took sacramental form to dwell within the communicant.

Medieval English theological and devotional works also reflect the belief that the sacrament manifests the Word itself and the Word's universe-changing powers. The Constitutions of 1237 of Alexander de Stavensby, bishop of Coventry, contains a provision for the ringing of a bell at the elevation of the Host.

> This bell will be like a small trumpet announcing the coming of the Judge, or rather of our Saviour, secretly; so that our souls may exult when we draw near to the heavenly banquet, with a threefold joy, for where our LORD's flesh is, there is His Soul, and there is GOD the Word.[50]

The thirteenth-century *Ancrene Riwle* prescribes as a prayer to the elevated Host the following formula: "Ecce salus mundi. uerbum patris. hostia uere uiua caro deitas integra uerus homo [Here is the health of the world, the Word of the Father, true sacrifice, living flesh of the God-Man.]"[51]

The perception of the sacrament as Word, the creative Logos, is also reflected in a manuscript of about 1400, in a tract headed: "Here sueþ a preciouse mater, how a man schal make hym cleer and perfite clene biforne þe resseyuynge of þe sacramente of þe auter." The tract's author points out that what the communicant receives is "soþely ihesu crist—sooþfaste god and man, þat made all þing of nouȝtte."[52] Similarly, John Lydgate, in his fifteenth-century poem, *Merita Missae*, adjures his readers to consider, at the end of Mass, the nature of what they have seen: "Than haste thoue sene that coste the noȝt, / The kyng that all thys world hathe wroȝt, / The kyng that mad bothe day and nyght."[53]

The Word's power and progression and the Word-sacrament equation also appear in the English vernacular lyric. One fifteenth-century carol begins with these lines:

> Whan nothyng was but God alone,
> The Fader, the Holy Gost, with the Son,
> On was iii, and iii was On.
>   What is this why?
> To frayn why I hold but foly;
> It is non other sertenly
> But virtus verbi Domini [the virtue of God's Word].[54]

The last four lines are repeated as conclusion to each of the carol's six verses. The second opens with the line, " 'Fiat' was a word ful bold"; this and the two following verses describe Creation as effected by the Word. Verse five, alluding to a miracle attributed to Bede, characterizes the response God's Word evokes from his creatures: "Whan Bede had prechyd to the stonys dry, / The myght of God mad hem to cry, / 'Amen!' Certys, this is no ly." It is the final verse of the carol that, like the Corpus Christi liturgy, sets forth the Eucharist as a manifestation of God's Word.

> Herytykes wonder of this thyng most:
> How God is put in the holy Host,
> Her and at Rome and in euery cost.
>   What is why?
> To frayne why I hold it but foly;
> It is non other certenly
> But virtus verbi Domini.

Not surprisingly, polemicists against Lollardy drew heavily upon the orthodox theology here documented. Stressing the central and miraculous importance of the Eucharist as, so to speak, God's last Word, they wielded a powerful weapon against heresy.

Netter, in the *Doctrinale Fidei*, specifically uses the Word-sacrament equation to counter Wyclif's sacramental heresy.

> Ecce Christus in nobis per hoc sacramentum manet corporaliter: non autem corporaliter corporalitate panis, . . . sed carnis, in qua Verbum caro factum est. Et secundum hanc carnem item naturaliter in nobis manet, & non per consensum tantummodo voluntatis. Numquid pecco, si inferam: ergo non tantum spiritualiter, sed etiam corporaliter, naturaliter, & carnaliter manducatur? Nam sicut dixisti supra, hoc est spiritualiter illam comedere escam, per amorem in Christo manere: non sic autem tantummodo Christus per voluntatis consensum, sed etiam corporaliter, carnaliter manducatur; ergo item carnaliter, & non tantum spiritualiter manducatur. [Christ abides in us bodily through this Sacrament, but not bodily by the bodily character of bread, . . . but of the flesh, in which the Word was made flesh. And according to this flesh also He abides in us naturally, and not only by the consent of the will. Do I sin then if I add, therefore not only spiritually, but also bodily, naturally, and carnally He is eaten? For as you [Wyclif] said above, to eat this food spiritually is to abide in Christ by love; but Christ is eaten not only in this way by the consent of the will, but also corporally and carnally; therefore He is eaten carnally and not only spiritually.][55]

Netter's work, although a learned and thorough refutation of Lollardy, could not directly influence the laity. Other documents, however, had this power. One of the most important anti-Lollard tracts addressed to the laity was Nicholas Love's *The Mirrour of the blessyd lyf of Jesu Christ* (ca. 1410). This work belongs to the genre of "Lives of Christ," a genre to which Martin Stevens, significantly, would also assign the Corpus Christi cycles. Indeed, as Stevens points out, Love's *Mirrour* was one of the sources of the N-Town cycle.[56] The work's use was authorized by Archbishop Thomas Arundel, who had been for some time preoccupied with the problem of Lollardy. As Margaret Deanesly notes, his authorization, including the statement that "he did it 'to the confuting of all false Lollards and heretics,' suggests a counter-move to the Lollard efforts to publish the gospels in English."[57] The book, whose rapid rise to popularity must have gratified Arundel, was a translation of the *Meditationes vitae Christi*, then attributed to Bonaventure. Its translator, Love, was prior of the Carthusian monastery of Mount Grace at Ingleby, Yorkshire, which may support the possibility that northern anti-Lollard efforts were especially vital.

The work is divided into seven parts. The first six, headed "Moneday" through "Saturday," begin with the depiction of a heavenly council concerning redemption, proceed to the life of Mary and the Incarnation, and then describe Christ's life, death, and post-Resurrection appearances to the Apostles. The concluding and indeed climactic portion of the work is a treatise on the Eucharist. As Deanesly suggests, Love "met the Lollards on their own ground" in the body of the tract, since the Lollard Bible translators asserted that "their aim was simply to popularise the connected story of the 'meek and poor and charitable living of Christ' and His apostles."[58] But while the Lollard gospelers' emphasis was always on the ministry and the teachings, with an appeal to the reader's understanding, Love's version abridges just those portions, expanding instead on the miraculous and devotion-inspiring events: the Nativity, the Passion, the Resurrection, and the Ascension, in particular.[59]

This emphasis on the miraculous culminates in the treatise on the Eucharist, in which Lollard errors are specifically addressed. Love complains, "We haue seyn in oure dayes how the disciples of Antecrist / that ben cleped lollardes / hauen made moche dissencioun and diuisioun in holy chirche."[60] The treatise recalls the Corpus Christi liturgy in its discussion of the Word's power.

> Hit is a ful greet merueyle that by vertue of cristes wordes brede is turned in to goddes body / and wyne in to his blode. And to strengthe vs in byleue of tis merueyle we schole haue in mynd that he with the self myȝt of his worde made all the world of nouȝt, and of the ribbe of Adam made Eue in flesche and blood, and turnede the wyf of loth in to an ymage of salte, and moyses ȝerde tornede in to a serpente, and the welles and wateres of Egipte turnede in to blode. Wherfore sithen god all myȝty wrouȝte alle these merueyles and many moo aboue the resoun of man and the comune curse of kynde, why may he not also by the self myȝt turne brede in to his body? There is non resoun to preue the contraire but if we wolde seie that god were not all myȝti / that god forbede.[61]

In its treatment of both scriptural material and sacramental theology, the *Mirrour* conveys the same message we have seen in the *Lay-Folks Mass-Book*: God's Word reaches Christians through his miracles, chief among which is the sacrament of the Mass.

The emphasis on miracle as central to Christian faith and life also appears in another of the Church's countermeasures against Lollardy. Cutts asserts that the heresy-fighting Church

> had recourse to the old, old, appeal of miracles as a last and irrefutable proof of its dogmas. It was a method thoroughly approved by

those who, like Roger Dymmok, wrote in refutation of the Wycliffite views and complained that the Lollards branded the miracles as false and refused to give them credence. . . . Though they might not bring back those who had already deserted, there was hope of strengthening the faith of the others, and old miracles were recounted and new ones multiplied and related to the glory of that faith.[62]

Cutts documents the recounting of such miracles on several occasions from the 1380s to the 1460s;[63] the earliest of these is representative and merits our attention. In 1382, during the period of the Blackfriars' Council that condemned Wyclif's doctrines, a Lollard, Sir Cornelius de Clone, experienced a miraculous vision: "In fractione vero hostiae miles respexit et vidit oculo suo corporali in manibus fratris celebrantis veram carnem, crudam, et sanguinolentam divisam in tres partes"[64] (on the breaking of the host the knight saw with his bodily eyes in the hands of the officiating friar true bleeding flesh . . . divided into three parts).[65] Such bleeding Host miracles are frequent in devotional literature from the twelfth century on, and it is not surprising to see them reappear in this context. Sir Cornelius was fully converted from his heretical leanings. He had received a potent message through the channel defined by orthodox theology: God's Word reached him through the sacrament.

*   *   *

Like the documents I have been discussing, the Towneley cycle could function as a counter to Lollard heresy through a focus on God's Word, a theology on which the orthodox and the heretics were most at odds. Kendall's analysis of the origins of the opposition is illuminating. Over time, "as the immediacy of the experience [of the Eucharist] became gradually lost to the commoner, alternative means of reaffirming spiritual community arose: Lollardy, with its rational mystery of truth tried, offered a radical substitution, the medieval cycles, a more orthodox one. *The Plaie called Corpus Christi*, as its name implies, presents a direct dramatic analogue to eucharistic worship." Like Love's *Mirrour*, the cycles "met the Lollards on their own ground" in offering just what the Lollards offered—only more attractively packaged: "a program of biblical instruction: a series of dramatic, vernacular sermons drawn from scripture, often with expositors carefully policing the interpretive response of the spectator."[66] Stressing sacramentality, reiterating the equation between God's Word and the Eucharist, the Towneley plays could serve not only to fortify the spectators in orthodoxy but also quite specifically to counter Lollardy. As I have shown, two issues dominated Lollard belief: they questioned—or denied—the doctrine of transubstantiation, and they insisted upon the dissemination of God's Word to the faithful, through preaching and, above all, through the translation of the Bible into English. Orthodox theologies of the Word and the sacrament provided rebuttals to these views, and these rebuttals could be embodied not only polemically but also dramatically.

If the cycles are to be considered as embodying an answer to Lollardy, it is important to recognize just how satisfying an answer they could be. Spiritual hunger appears to have been a common condition in late medieval England, and it was a condition to which both the Lollards and the playwrights seem to have been responsive. Travis's discussion of the cycles' cultural role is especially insightful. As he sees it, the cycles emphasized communion, community, and sense experience of the sacred: "Like the eucharistic Host itself, late medieval drama attempted a far-reaching unification of the sacred and the secular, of Christ and the community of the faithful." In so doing, the drama— along with other "sacred actions," including the Mass and the Corpus Christi feast and procession—"gratified in different ways . . . a cluster of similar religious and psychological needs. . . . [Each] . . . was a sacred action demonstrating the community's need to become at one with Christ by offering visible proof of Christ's physical presence."[67] As Kendall's analysis suggests, Lollardy recognized the cultural need for an intensification of spiritual experience and responded to that need in its way. But Lollardy was disputatious and defensive, an attack on the status quo rather than an affirmation of the existing community. Although Lollardy sought to appease the hunger for ritual and mystical experience in its ritualization of biblical study, through which inspiration was to be attained, it offered strenuous and primarily intellectual solutions—the struggle toward spiritual truth through intensive study of the Bible—and denied the validity of aesthetic and affective ones. The spiritually enhanced orthodoxy of which the cycles are an outgrowth promised not only spiritual food more easily attained but stability, serenity, and pleasures for the heart and the senses—not least of which were to be derived from the believer's immediate proximity to the living Christ.

All the extant Corpus Christi cycles flourished in a socially and theologically contentious climate. It is possible that close examination of the York, Chester, and N-Town plays would also result in discoveries of counter-Lollard potency. This analysis of the Towneley plays is intended to open, not to complete, a line of inquiry. However, the Towneley cycle is a particularly good starting point for the inquiry because of its revisions and additions at the hand of the Wakefield Master.[68] It is his work that has attracted the greatest attention to the cycle, and Stevens makes a compelling argument for our viewing him not as one author-reviser among many, but as the "Wakefield Author": "the principal compiler and the guiding intelligence of the Wakefield cycle."[69] The Wakefield Master's contributions were made during a period fraught with heretical upheaval, and it will be demonstrated that the Master's plays—and, indeed, the powerfully unified cycle in which his work resulted—manifest sharply counter-Lollard themes and techniques. While it cannot be proven that the playwright's intention was specifically counter-Lollard, a strong case can be made that the cycle had that effect for some part of its audience—that there *was* a counter-Lollard Towneley cycle in the minds of some of its spectators. Although speculation on authorial intention is at times irresistible, my primary intention, in the pages that follow, is to describe not what the playwright did, but what the *cycle* could have done to and for its audience.

In part 2, I will begin my examination of the Towneley plays with a test case, the *Mactacio Abel,* the cycle's Cain and Abel play. Many critics believe the Wakefield Master to be among the author-revisers of this play; some would attribute it to him in toto.[70] Stevens sees the play as an encapsulization of the cycle's perspective.[71] The demonstration in chapter 3 of this play's embodiment of counter-Lollard material will provide a foundation for the later chapters' analyses of the cycle's other episodes.

Chapter 4 looks both backward and forward from the vantage point of the *Mactacio Abel* to provide an overview of the Old Testament plays' concern with the theme of God's Word as it was successively transmitted to patriarchs and prophets in the ages before its incarnation and subsequent sacramental fulfillment. This chapter also examines the cycle's proclericalism: its presentation of Old Testament worthies as protopriests who transmit God's Word from within a liturgically and sacramentally defined setting. These protopriests also engage in polemics with their adversaries, who are often given Lollard traits. The debaters provide the audience with resonant models of appropriate and inappropriate responses to the Word.

Chapter 5, on the infancy plays, and 6, on Christ's teachings and his Passion, demonstrate how the doctrine of transubstantiation finds powerful dramatic embodiment in the cycle. In these plays, "real," living Christ is portrayed in sacramental terms. From the moment of the Nativity on, Christ is presented simultaneously in terms of his life's linear progression and in the context of the language, actions, and imagery of the sacrifice of the Mass. The plays work to convince the audience intellectually of the Real Presence's truth, while at the same time they reassert the overwhelming emotional power of Christ's presence among his believers at Mass. As Travis puts it, the cycle drama was "on the verge of being seen as embodying the reality it imitated. . . . The audience is called upon to perform an imagined role as communicants in a sacred act, and to feel after participating in that act that their souls have been cleansed."[72]

In chapters 7 and 8, I discuss the plays that bring the audience beyond Christ's earthly life. The Word that effected Creation, spoke to the patriarchs and prophets, and was incarnated and sacrificed, now is seen directly in its sacramental fulfillment. God's Word continues to speak, now through the Eucharist, and the audience perceives their own sacramental observance in a new and powerful light. Their new vision affects them in the present and, as chapter 8 shows, in the future, the day of Judgment. They embrace the continuum of salvific history in which the Word and the sacrament are one. The end of the cycle leaves them edified and powerfully fortified against Lollardy.

Part 2
The Cycle Enacts the Sacrament

3
The Case of Cain

While the Lollards inveighed against neglectful priests and labored to translate the Bible, the Church responded from the foundation of its broader definition of the Word of God. Orthodoxy held that the Word is to be found not only in Scripture, but also in the Church's vast system of commentary, doctrine, and ritual use, a system requiring the priest's mediation. Without a knowledge of that "second half" of the faith, the would-be exegete—the Lollard layman, for example—would inevitably go astray. The Word of God reaches the people through all the Church's official writings, pronouncements, and actions, most directly—under clerical auspices—through the Mass and the sacraments. What the Lollards were trying to do was, to the orthodox way of thinking, already being done in the only possible way. The Towneley cycle, reflecting its times and its orthodox authorship, expresses this point of view and forwards this program. Upholding clerical authority and validating sacramentality, the cycle brings God's Word to the people and teaches them proper responses. It evinces the Word's power and shows the identity among its several forms: God's speech in the Old Testament, prophecy, the Word Incarnate, and—especially—the Eucharistic Presence.

I take as my test case the cycle's second play, the *Mactacio Abel*, a play that bears signs of the Wakefield Master's hand and that modern readers have found intriguing and effective. But what of medieval spectators?—people of all ranks, many of them knowingly caught in the cross fire of orthodox-heterodox contestation. If we bring to the examination of this play an awareness of the issues to which these debates sensitized members of the original audience, what will we see in the Towneley Cain and Abel play? I would suggest that we find in this drama an encapsulization of some of the cycle's best techniques both of strengthening orthodoxy and of countering Lollard heresy. The play evokes the audience's liturgical experience and in so doing presents a "priest" as the vehicle of God's Word. Thus bolstering orthodoxy while—through Cain's characterization—countering Lollard views of tithing, of mendicancy, and of conscience, the play functions as a dramatically effective counter-Lollard force.

Let us begin with Abel's entrance and the delivery of what is, significantly, his longest speech in the play. He begins:

> . . . leif brother, here my sawe—
> It is the custom of oure lawe,
> All that wyrk as the wise
> shall worship god with sacrifice.
>
> (68–71)

Abel's "sawe" (saying), stating divine law, embodies God's Word. Abel, who in his act of oblation is a familiar type of the priest at Mass, is priestlike throughout the play as a mouthpiece of God's Word in a figurally ecclesiastical setting. Cain's opposition to him has therefore an anticlerical coloring, and his verbal battles with Abel suggest Lollard-like unwillingness to "hear" God's Word from such a source.

The scene also works through anachronism—a "two-way mirror," as Stevens terms it[1]—to invoke the spectators' experience at Mass, reminding them of the connection between the Real Presence and their personal salvation. The playwright presents the idea of sacrifice in such a way that it applies less directly to Cain and Abel than to the spectators themselves. Abel says, "Then blis withoutten end / get we for oure seruyce, / of hym that is oure saulis leche" (81–83). The "saulis leche" is Christ, and Abel himself will have to wait "foure thousand winter"[2] for the Harrowing of Hell to reap his reward of bliss. The audience, however, participate in the sacrifice of the Mass, a sacrifice—by virtue of the Real Presence—of and by their "saulis leche"; and they hope for rather more immediate heavenly bliss. Although Abel's statement is true of his own ultimate experience, it is more immediately true of the Mass, and the medieval audience was well grounded to recognize Abel's offering as a type of the liturgical sacrifice.

That Abel's speech has contemporary liturgical implications is accentuated by Cain's response: "How! let furth youre geyse, the fox will preche; / How long wilt thou me appech / With thi sermonyng?" (84–86). He insinuates that his priestlike brother is trying to manipulate and cheat him with words: Cain will not acknowledge the divine source of "sermonyng" language. The playwright conflates the ideas of sacrifice and tithing, permitting Cain to voice further distrust of established religion. While tithes were used in the upkeep of the church and the reasonable maintenance of the clergy, their most important purpose, from a doctrinal standpoint, was the relief of the poor. When Cain complains, "My farthyng is in the preest hand / syn last tyme I offryd" (104–5), he purports to be criticizing clerical corruption.

Cain's words smack of Lollardy. To be sure, the Lollards were not the only unwilling tithers in late medieval England.[3] The Lollard position on tithing, however, is strikingly similar to Cain's, although Cain's becomes parodic. In the Lollard tract entitled "Sixteen Points on which the Bishops accuse Lollards," the third item is "þat no man is holdoun to tiþe in manere nowe vsed of þe chirche, but suche tiþis and offiri[n]gis be þe lawe of God schuld be deled to þe pore nedi men."[4] The tract's author counters this accusation, asserting that the Lollards acknowledge the laws of tithing, but it adds this proviso concerning the priests to whom tithes are paid: "if þei lyuen as curatis schulden, and spenden þe goodis of þe chirche to Goddis worschippe in hemself and oþur pore puple, þane ben þe tiþus paied to þe pore men and nedi, for þei hemself ben pore."[5] Implicit in this reasonable defense is a Lollard doctrine of tithing that the Church found reprehensible, that is, that tithes should be withheld from a priest deemed neglectful and might be allocated at the tither's discretion. In 1425, the Lollard William Russell argued that "personal tithes did not fall under divine law, at least the payment of them to a parish clergyman, and that anyone could dispose of them to pious uses for the poor."[6] Questioning his responsibility for tithing, adducing the venality of the priest, Cain aligns himself with the heretics. Although his position becomes a travesty when he implies that he will be the sole beneficiary of his own charity, the Lollards too were open to the charge that their antitithing stance was selfishly motivated. Cain is thus Lollard-like in failing to recognize God's presence in the anachronistic church and choosing to see only a corrupt priest.

In this scene Cain shows yet another Lollard bias. Self-righteously he declares to Abel that he has better, more important things to do than to complete the ritual: "Shuld I leife my plogh & all thyng / And go with the to make offeryng? / Nay! thou fyndys me not so mad!" (91–93). Cain implies that he is dedicated to his hard work, albeit for pragmatic reasons, and that

Abel is recommending irresponsible behavior. Later in the altercation, Cain reinforces his position by suggesting that his way of life will preserve him from the ignominy of begging.

> ffor had I giffen away my goode,
> then myght I go with a ryffen hood,
> And it is better hold that I haue
> then go from doore to doore & craue.
>
> (140–43)

Interestingly, while "craue" means "beg," the word is also used in the context of a sinner's begging for mercy. Exalting the virtue of labor over devotion, Cain might be a mouthpiece of Wyclif himself. As Trevelyan states, Wyclif's "assertion of the superiority of an active over a devotional life was in that age a daring rebellion. It startled and scandalised churchmen; for half the Church institutions were based on the assumption that prayer and praise were better than work in the world."[7] Wyclif's attitude became central to the Lollard attack on the priesthood, and Lollard writings frequently contrast the freeloading of worldly priests and clerical mendicants with the hard labor of "trewe" men.[8] This contrast also appears in the *Jack Upland* versified polemical series. The orthodox Friar Daw Topias replies to Lollard Jack's first sally with a downgrading of laborers in favor of priests.

> Alþouȝ Poul in his pistele laborers preisiþ,
> Displese him not þe preestes þat syngen her masses.
> For riȝt as in þi bodi Iake, ben ordeyned þin hondis,
> For þin heed, & for þi feet, & for þin eyen to wirken—
> Riȝ so þe comoun peple God haþ disposid,
> To laboren for Holi Chirche & lordshipis also.[9]

But in Jack's view, the friar is merely twisting words.

> Me merueliþ of þi lewdnes, Dawe—or of wilful lesynges—
> For Poule laborid with his hondes, & oþer postilles also—
> ȝee, oure gentil Iesu, as it is opunly knowe.[10]

Like Cain, Jack would argue that manual labor is more valuable than the works of the friars. Friars, after all, are beggars who assert the lawfulness of begging, while Lollard tracts take Cain's position, that begging is censurable.

Also freris seyn and mayntenan, þat begginge is leveful, þo whiche is dampned by God, bothe in þo Olde Testament and in þo New. For in þo fyveȝt boke of holy writt, God seis to his puple, Algatis a nedy mon and begger schal not be amonge ȝowe. . . . Also Crist biddes his apostils and his disciplis, þat þei schul not bere a sachel ne scrippe bot loke what meyneȝ is hable to here þe gospel, and eete and drinke þerinne, and passe not þennes, and not passe fro hous to hous. . . . Also Seynt Clement ordeyned þat Cristen men schulden not begg opunly. And, for to putt awey þis beggynge, Seynt Austyne makes twoo bokes, hou munkis owen to travel wiþ her hondis for her lyvelode. And þo same techis Benett to his munkis, and Seynt Bernarde; and so does Fraunceys to freris.[11]

So Cain's assertions of his dignity as a laborer and his desire to avoid beggary, while apparently elevated and laudable sentiments, place him in dangerous company.

As the play continues, the brothers proceed to the sacrifice, although Cain never stops battling the religious authority Abel personifies. Not only does Cain attempt to invalidate what Abel represents by silencing him, he also urges his brother to emulate him. In a burst of ironic fraternal advice, Cain counsels Abel, "Chaunge thi conscience, as I do myn, / yit teynd thou not thi mesel swyne?" (263–64). That is, Cain argues that the conscience is merely a tool, and an adjustable one at that. He suggests that Abel would do well to adjust his in such a way that he could be comfortable in tithing his "mesel" (diseased) animals. Here again, Cain can be seen as a caricature of a Lollard. While orthodox writers discussed conscience as an *effect* of the individual's behavior—something that was or was not "clene" as a result of actions or inactions, the Lollards viewed conscience as rather a *cause* of behavior, a touchstone to be used in the personal determination of what was right. From the viewpoint of the authoritarian Church, such a notion of conscience was dangerous, and "men of conscience" were suspect. One Wycliffite tract suggests that men ought to obey man-made law—which would include much that the Church enforced—only "in as myche as þei witen þat it acordiþ wiþ goddis lawe & reson & good conscience."[12] Wyclif himself, in the tract "Of Confession," uses the phrase "men of conscience" to refer to those, his followers, who need not confess to a priest.[13] Cain the "man of conscience," like Cain the hardworking farmer, shows his affinity with the Lollards.

When Cain attempts to burn his measly offering, nature itself opposes his efforts. Frustrated by his ineffectuality, Cain turns his anger against Abel. It is at this point that God first speaks, although he may have been visible to the audience and to Abel—but not to Cain—since the play's opening. God repeats Abel's exhortations to proper tithing, making it clear that Abel has been functioning as a sanctioned vehicle of the Word. As God takes Abel's part against Cain in the ongoing verbal battle, Cain's response is strategic blasphemy.

> Whi, who is that hob-ouer-the-wall?
> we! who was that that piped so small?
> Com go we hens, for perels all;
> God is out of hys wit.

(297–300)

In God's presence and addressed by his Word, Cain attacks the Word by belittling it, asserting his own word against God's. One imagines the actor, a cupped hand to his ear, miming his inability to hear the voice that "piped so small." But this is merely an extension of Cain's earlier belittling of the Word when the priestly Abel was its vehicle. The point is made that Cain in a sense truly does not hear God's Word, for he refuses to recognize its power, its ubiquity, and its sovereignty over him.

After he murders Abel, Cain compounds his sinfulness by denying the efficacy of prayer: "It is no boyte mercy to crauve, / ffor if I do I mon none haue" (376–77). Once again, he refuses to be a beggar, and again it is because of his own imagined superiority. Rather than using language to invoke God's power, Cain, sinfully "self-sufficient," asserts in his defense the powers of his own word. He hopes to undo his deed by denying it, and he enlists Garcio, his anachronistic servant, in the cause. In the stichomythic dialogue that ensues, the ineffectuality of Cain's self-pardon is accentuated as Garcio undercuts his every phrase.

> Caym. I command you in the kyngis nayme,
> Garcio. And in my masteres, fals Cayme,
> Caym. That no man at thame fynd fawt ne blame.
> Garcio. Yey, cold rost is at my masteres hame.
>
> Caym. Nowther with hym nor with his knafe,
> Garcio. What, I hope my master rafe.
> Caym. ffor thay are trew, full many fold;
> Garcio. My master suppys no coyle bot cold.

(418–25)

"Trew" is a descriptor the Lollards very often claimed for them-selves,[14] and like Cain, they tended to assert their claim to it through contentious argumentation.

As this dialogue continues, Garcio's several references to his hunger (427, 429, 431) hark back to the play's earlier indications that Cain has been a force of disruption in his small social world and has perverted the created hierarchy. In the opening scene, prior to Abel's entrance, the spectators learned that Garcio had failed to feed the animals; they now understand that Garcio's negligence was a repercussion of Cain's failure to feed him. As Cain has been disobedient to his master, he has also failed to be a good master in his own appointed station. A good master feeds his servants: it is significant that Abel, a pastoral exemplum, is concerned with his beasts' having enough to eat (308–10). The Towneley cycle, here and elsewhere, characterizes the perverted hierarchy of fallen humanity by the hunger of dependent crea-tures. The meaning of this characterization is amplified in a contemporary poem that suggests liturgical and sacramental sig-nificance.

> Men suld be bowsum in thare mode,
> And gladly go to *gostly fode,*
> That es to say to *goddes worde*
> That prechares gaders of goddes horde.[15]

The phrase "gostly fode" is also frequently employed in homi-letic poetry to describe the Eucharist itself.[16]

Garcio, cut off from God's Word, hungers literally, as a result of a bad master's neglect. Further—mirroring, in all probability, the condition of many of the spectators—he is spiritually hungry. Such hunger cannot be appeased in the service of the anticlerical Cain. Garcio is in need of "gostly fode," not only in its homiletic form, but also in those liturgical and sacramental embodiments the Lollards called into question. Garcio himself does not recog-nize the spiritual dimension of his hunger, but the audience would have understood it. Evoked in the emotionally laden con-text of Abel's sacrifice and murder—types, respectively, of the Eucharist and the Passion—Garcio's hunger points most directly to the orthodox stance on fallen humanity's need for the re-demptive sacrament of the Real Presence. Indeed Garcio is both hungry and thirsty—perhaps a suggestion of the dual species of the sacrament—and his "stomak is redy to receyfe" (431), a verb associated with sacramental communion. The sacrament's devotional power was, finally, the Church's most potent weapon against Lollardy, and this play participates in the cycle's dramatic embodiment of that power.

The Towneley Cain, with his specifically Lollard anticlerical views and his fatal antagonism toward his priestlike brother, instructs the spectators in the dangers of Lollardy. His function as an instructor—a sort of anti-Expositor—is ironically pointed up in his closing speech, in which he promises Garcio, "I shall, if I may, / Tech the another lore" (453–54). Appearing, in the early part of the play, to share the woes of the hardworking farmers in the audience, Cain is initially attractive in his independent spirit and his opposition to clerical corruption. But the spectators must dissociate from Cain and reject his "lore" as he moves from an apparently reformist stance to blasphemy and to murder. Having severed the bond of their identification with Cain, the play's viewers are less likely, in the future, to be attracted to such doctrines and disruptive attitudes as Cain represents. They have been empowered with skepticism that could function well against Lollardy. Equally importantly, they have been shown the attractions of orthodoxy: social stability contrasted with lawlessness and disruption; Abel's serenity contrasted with Cain's dissatisfaction and explosive anger; fruitfulness and repletion contrasted with sterility and hunger; and God's approbation and protection contrasted with his curse.

4

Priests and Polemics

The priest—under attack by the Lollards as both corrupt and unnecessary—is the hero of the *Mactacio Abel*. Indeed, throughout the cycle, priest figures like Abel contribute to the drama's counter-Lollard force. Portrayed as the vehicles of God's Word, in large part through their role as custodians of ritual and sacrament, these characters voice doctrine as they debate with heretics and sinners. Bringing before us a procession of scriptural protopriests, the Towneley plays fortify the spectators against the anticlericalism that Lollardy was making dangerously popular.

The cycle begins, appropriately, with the Word of God: a ten-stanza monologue in which God accomplishes the work of the first five days of Creation. He is the source of all things, he tells the audience.

> All maner thyng is in my thoght,
> Withoutten me there may be noght,
>   ffor all is in my sight;
> hit shall be done after my will,
> that I haue thoght I shall fulfill
>   And manteyn with my might.

(13–18)

Speaking in the present tense, God effects Creation with his Word: "It shall be," he stresses, "as I say" (27). Although Abel is the cycle's first human priest figure, even the good angels of the *Creation* play are endowed with priestly attributes. The Cherubim, enacting a devotional ritual, mediate between God and the spectators as the priest mediates at Mass. They provide a model of worshipful response to the Creator.

> Oure lord god in trynyte,
> Myrth and lovyng be to the,
> Myrth and lovyng ouer all thyng;
> ffor thou has made, with thi bidyng,

Heuen, & erth, and all that is,
and giffen vs Ioy that neuer shall mys.

(61–66)

The angels are also priestlike in that they teach specific tenets of doctrine. Even the most remiss parish priest is not likely to have neglected to instruct his parishioners in the Apostles' Creed, which, like the angelic paean, begins with a statement of belief in God's act of creation ex nihilo, God's prototypical use of the Word to bring about reality.

As the good angels are priestlike, so Lucifer is certainly heretical. He claims the "mastre" (81) that is God's alone, attempting to imitate God's Word and wield the power it embodies. His heresy is comparable to that of the Lollard who, translating the Bible, would arrogate God's Word. Such a comparison might be intended; it is warranted by no less a figure than John Gower, who, in one of his Latin poems, compares Wyclif to Satan and suggests that the devil must be behind Lollard heresy.[1] While the Cherubim have addressed God in couplets, Lucifer speaks in a stanza modeled on that spoken by God but increasingly flawed as his speech continues.[2] As the stanza form breaks down, the speech becomes repetitive and strident, and Lucifer becomes increasingly less attractive. The attempted imitation itself reveals Lucifer's failure to acknowledge God's Word and the creaturely status it has granted him. In attempting to seize God's power, Lucifer imitates the form, not the essence, of his language. He issues commands—"master ye shall me call" (98)—but his words, unlike the deity's, do not effect what they express. The spectators see that evil response to God's Word may take the form of imitative but ultimately empty language. Biblical words, translated by the Lollards but unsanctioned by the Church, would have just such a hollow resonance to orthodox ears.

Lucifer's claims initiate the conflict of good and evil that only the completed cycle will resolve. The angels' debate is a battle of words in which each side strives to silence the other. In response to a bad angel's support of Lucifer, the second good angel says, "I reyde ye sese of that ye sayn, / ffor well I wote ye carpe in vayne" (114–15). He accuses his adversary precisely of empty speech, words that will see no fulfillment in deeds. The second bad angel counters with "hold thy peasse" (122), and the linguistic battle is underway. This is the first of numerous instances in the cycle in which heretical characters assert themselves verbally over priestlike vehicles of God's Word.

Martin Stevens—in his 1977 *Speculum* article, "Language as Theme in the Wakefield Plays," and in his 1987 book, *Four Middle English Mystery Cycles*—brilliantly analyzes the role of language in the cycle, from Lucifer's flawed stanza in the *Creation* play to the function of the devil Tutivillus in the dramatization of the Last Judgment. As he sees it, the theme of language use and abuse unifies the cycle, and "we owe this focus to the Wakefield author as reviser and compiler of the cycle. . . . The Wakefield author is pervasively concerned with 'vayn carpyng,' . . . with the abuse of language, especially by those who oppose God." Stevens connects this concern with the dramatized conflict between heavenly and earthly laws and discusses the role of the "loquacious tyrant figure." Yet as Stevens also recognizes, these tyrants are by no means invariably persons of high stature or civil authority; in addition to kings and procurators and high priests, they also include "soldiers, shepherds, shrewish wives." Their interlocutors speak simply or, finally, in the case of Jesus in the Passion sequence, not at all: they are vehicles of the Word. Stevens speaks of the playwright's "overriding concern with the falsity of man's word as contrasted with the Word."[3]

I disagree with Stevens very little indeed. However, my substitution of *heretics* for Stevens's *tyrants* is more than a simple semantic shift. My term accounts for the considerable diversity in class and power among these characters and highlights what Stevens also recognizes—that the opponents of God's Word are not necessarily, and sometimes not at all, puffed up by their ephemeral possession of worldly authority. What gives them their hubris is something more insidious, a belief in their own intrinsic superiority over those in the clerical establishment. Only people of the upper classes can, strictly speaking, be "tyrants"—Stevens in fact refers to Noah's Uxor as an "unlikely" tyrant figure[4]—while heresy, Lollardy in particular, infiltrated society at all levels.

As I will demonstrate, the cycle's debate between priests and heretics concerning the source and nature of truth mirrors the period's polemical writings pro- and anti-Lollard. Lollards, as discussed in chapter 2, asserted that priests forbade their parishioners to know God's Word and that they, the Lollards, would rectify this abuse. The contemporary orthodox homilist answered this claim with the assertion that the Church never forbade its members to "entermette of holywritte," but only forbade them to "mysvse" it.[5] The orthodox Church would argue, as becomes increasingly clear in the cycle, that it permitted and encouraged free access to "holywritt," the Word of God, and that its heretical opponents were the obfuscators and abusers of the Word.

As polemical upholders of new beliefs, the Lollards' words were inevitably many and much in evidence. DeWelles notes that anti-Lollard writers were "obsessed with one of the heretics' most powerful weapons—words, especially spoken words."[6] Indeed, the heretics earned for themselves the name of "janglers" (chatterers). An anti-Lollard poem of the fifteenth century pointedly refers to Lollard preaching as "janglyng."

> þer þe bibell is al myswent,
>   To iangle of Iob or Ieremye,
> þat construen hit after her entent
>   for lewd lust of lollardie.[7]

Another important document is the orthodox response, "Friar Daw's Reply," to the Lollard poem, "Jack Upland." The friar calls his Lollard opponent Jack a "jangler."

> Þow jawdewyne, þou jangeler, how stande þis to gider?
> . . . .
> Iak, se now þin errour & sumtyme sesse for shame,
> For þou jangelist as a jay & woost not what þou meenest.

To be sure, Jack turns the accusation around in his own rejoinder, which is full of accusations against Daw of blabbering and lying,[8] and this pattern is repeated in the cycle whenever heretical characters—Lucifer, Cain, and their followers—accuse their virtuous interlocutors of "carpyng" and "janglyng." All of this bears a striking resemblance to what Kendall presents as a pervasive dynamic in Lollard polemic.

> Lollardy as a theological outlook demanded the ritual of ideological combat. A religion of divisive extremes, Lollardy attempted to resolve the struggle of its internal contradictions [such as its reliance upon subjectivity in defining the "objective truth" of Scripture] by projecting that struggle outward into the public arena. By playing out their subjective dilemma in the field of objective action, by attacking in their enemies those elements of dogma and practice they feared in themselves, they managed to maintain a delicate inward balance.[9]

But orthodoxy stood firm on its assertion—an assertion that requires fewer and fewer words from the virtuous characters as the cycle goes on—that it was the Lollards and other heretics who misused the Word; the Towneley *Iudicium* drives home the message. The devil Tutivillus, on his way to collect his quota of damned souls, announces himself as "master lollar," adding, "And of sich men I mell me."[10] Many of the damned with whom he has dealings are later further specified as various kinds of abusers of language.

Long before the *Iudicium*, the vociferous heretic takes his—and her—place on the Towneley stage. Following the *Mactacio Abel*, the *Processus Noe* reenacts the polemic with Noah in the priest's role and his wife cast as the heretic. This play is wholly the product of the Wakefield Master's authorship and was added to the cycle during a period of flourishing Lollard activity. Noah's opening monologue delineates his role as doctrinal educator, as he praises the triune Creator, recalling his works, and recounts the fall of the angels and that of Adam and Eve. Although Noah questions humanity's deservings, he does not fall into Cain's error of denying the value and effect of prayer.

> Bot yit will I cry / for mercy and call;
> Noe thi seruant, am I / lord ouer all!
> Therfor me and my fry / shal with me fall;
> saue from velany / and bryng to thi hall
> > In heuen;
> And kepe me from syn,
> This warld within;
> Comly kyng of mankyn,
> > I pray the here my stevyn!

(64–72)

Once again, the drama evokes the audience's liturgical experience. Noah's prayer paraphrases the final petitions of the *Pater Noster*, the familiar prayer through which the priest shepherded the congregation at every Mass. God appears immediately at these lines' conclusion. It is difficult to imagine a more striking dramatization of the efficacy of prayer and the powers of priesthood.

God commands Noah to build the ark, a vehicle of redemption for himself and his family. Here Noah's priestly role is enhanced, for the ark was exegetically understood to figure later vehicles of redemption, the cross and the church.[11] The play alludes to the first of these antitypes by having God command the making of a ship "of nayle and bord" (119). The command to construct "houses of offyce" (134) in the ark may be a punning reference to the second. While "house of office" was the term applied to pantries, stables, and other outbuildings, the divine service was also known as the "office." Perhaps even the command to "Anoynt" (127) the ship points to its ecclesiastical antitype, evoking the priest's anointing of the altar in a church's consecration. The emphasis in this play on the church as a building—an emphasis that will recur later in such plays as the *Purificacio Mcrie*, the *Pagina doctorum*, and the *Iohannes baptista*—has special relevance as a counter-Lollard element. Kendall suggests that "the Lollard tendency to deny Christ's physical presence in the elements of the altar was symptomatic of their sense of God's ultimate inaccessibility," and this same sense led to their move "away from the stone nave and its sacred space and toward Milton's temple of 'th' upright heart and pure.' "[12] With its stress on the church building, the cycle enhances its elevation of the priesthood housed and the rituals enacted there; it shows how venerable and divinely ordained was the building the Lollards scorned.

Of course Noah is not only to build the ark, he is also to fill it with the animals he "governs" and see to their feeding—"They must haue corn and hay, / And oder mete alway" (159–60)—as well as his own and his family's. Although these injunctions are biblical in origin, their appearance in the play sharpens the portrayal of a pastoral Noah. Unlike the human and animal dependents of Cain and other wicked characters, the dependents of the obedient Noah, a prototypical Good Shepherd, will have enough to eat. As the priest administers the nurturant Word, liturgical and sacramental, within the church's walls, so Noah feeds his dependents. There will be no hunger, physical or spiritual, in the ark.

Noah asks for and receives God's blessing before turning homeward. It appears that he needs blessing: the actual building of the ark is the least of his worries as he anticipates an encounter with his "tethee" (186) wife. His apprehension is well-founded, for Uxor challenges him immediately. On the most literal level her words are an attack on his familial sovereignty.[13] But her outburst also aligns her with heretics like Cain who contrast their own hard labor with clerical indolence:

> To dede may we dryfe / or lif for the,
>   ffor want.
> When we swete or swynk,
> thou dos what thou thynk,

Yit of mete and of drynk
haue we veray skant.

(193–98)

By suggesting that the family is hungry, Uxor's speech implies that Noah has failed in his obligation to his dependents, that he is an inadequate master—or pastor. It is worth pointing out in this context that one of the horrors some among the orthodox foresaw resulting from the Lollards' Englished Bible was that of women noisily engaged in their own versions of scriptural exegesis and doctrinal argumentation.[14] The irony of Uxor's accusation, of course, is that Noah's activities are directed toward providing not only for the family, but for the future of all humanity. Without even letting Noah tell his "tythyngis" (199), a word that is later in the cycle pointedly associated with the Word's incarnation, she begins to "jangle" about his defects. Her tirade—imbued with anticlerical coloring—thus prevents her from hearing God's Word. Noah's response, "We! hold thi tong, ram-skyt / or I shall the still" (217), despite its indelicacy, is consonant with his role as a priestly vehicle of God's Word to unwilling listeners.

The verbal battle quickly becomes physical, however, as it will, more intensely, in a later scene. But while God's Word is not at this time communicated to Uxor, it is by no means forgotten as Noah now exerts all his energies in the ark's construction. The scene vividly evokes Noah's human vulnerability, revealing at the same time the power God lends his willing servants to accomplish his will. Albeit Noah is a type of Christ, he is even more clearly a type of the parish priest. The task is not easy, but Noah perseveres, and the finished product is a source of gratification. Noah is not proud, however; he recognizes the Creator as the real shipwright: "Hym that maide all of noght / I thank oonly" (287–88).

Noah's work is still far from complete. To fulfill God's command, he must now communicate it to his wife and family. This time he succeeds in so doing; but Uxor balks again—at the church door, as it were. She refuses to enter, and neither entreaty nor threat touches her: "All in vayn ye carp" (360). She taunts her husband, saying, "Thise great wordis shall not flay me" (380). Yet she has enough faith in the power of her own words to continue her verbal assault on her husband, implicating women spectators in the attack.

Lord, I were at ese / and hertely full hoyll,
Might I onys haue a measse / of wedows coyll;

> ffor thi saull, without lese / shuld I dele penny doyll,
> so wold mo, no frese / that I se on this sole
>   of wifis that ar here,
> ffor the life that thay leyd,
> Wold thare husbandis were dede,
> ffor, as euer ete I brede,
>   So wold I oure syre were.

(388–96)

Again, on the literal level, Uxor is a stock shrewish wife. But there are allusions in this speech that ironically redound to Noah's credit. For the medieval spectators, who recognize that Noah is both a type of Christ and a prototypical priest, Uxor's wish for the death of "oure syre" becomes a wish for the death by which all humanity is made "hoyll," and her references to food ("measse," "ete . . . brede") take on teasing Eucharistic connotations.

Of course Uxor intends nothing so complimentary. Noah responds to the malicious "janglyng" she does intend, counseling the married men in the audience to chastise their wives for their unruly tongues. At this point, the play's physical battles assume a clear significance within its theological structure. A passage from the Middle English homiletic tract *Dives and Pauper* sharpens the analogy between cleric and head of household that the play has already developed.

> And Sent Austyn seith þat iche man in his owyn houshold schulde don þe offys of þe buschop in techinge & correctynge of comoun þingis. And chastysyng longyth nout only to þe buschop but to euery gouernour aftir his name & his degre, to þe pore man gouernynge his pore houshold, to þe riche man gouernynge his mene, to þe housebond gouernynge his wif, to þe fadir & þe moodir gouernynge her childryn.[15]

Countering antiauthoritarianism on multiple levels, the play's action serves its theological function. In this battle, as well as in his earlier encounter with Uxor, Noah is not abandoning his role as vehicle of God's Word to vent his frustration or, in the theatrical context, merely to provide amusement. On the contrary, he is fulfilling that "buschop's" role quite properly, chastising his subject wife when verbal instruction fails. The audience is reminded that clerical authority, too, might resort to force when education proved ineffectual: Lollards and other heretics might experience duress if they scorned opportunities to recant.

The battle ends, Uxor's "janglyng" ceases, and the action proceeds harmoniously to its divinely willed conclusion. As Stevens suggests, "If we bear in mind the figural interpretation of Noah and the ark, then the stillness and stability at the end of the play tell us something about the role of the church in a world too much obsessed with the discord of words."[16] With heretical debate stilled, Noah's priestly function refocuses on nurturance. His convert, Uxor, is the first to point beyond the flood to the succeeding reconciliation.

> Me thynk, bi my wit,
> the son shynes in the eest / lo, is not yond it?
> We shuld haue a good feest / were thise floodis flyt
> So spytus.
>
> (452–55)

J. R. R. Tolkien has suggested that these lines may incorporate an allusion to the Feast of Corpus Christi.[17] The allusion to a feast over which Noah will preside certainly suggests a corrective reordering of the created hierarchy in the flood's aftermath. Characterizing the redemption of Noah and his family, the "feest" also connotes the redemptive Eucharistic meal and the Church feast established in its honor. Significantly, the "good feest" depends upon the appearance of the "son." Uxor is once again an unconscious exegete. She provides the audience with a connection between the redemption she experiences—within the protochurch and under priestly auspices—and that for which they strive.

* * *

Heretical polemics—debates between priests and heretics—are absent from the next sequence of plays, the *Abraham*, the *Isaac*, and the *Jacob*. These plays, however, continue to characterize as priestlike those Old Testament patriarchs who received God's Word directly from its source. Invoking the audience's liturgical experiences, the plays refresh in the spectators' eyes the Church's sanctity and the priest's authority.

It is within a construct of powerful typological significance that the action of the *Abraham* unfolds. As a type of Christ's Passion, the sacrifice of Isaac is moving and instructive.[18] Abraham's agony and Isaac's terror greatly enhance the audience's appreciation of the sacrifice offered for their redemption and of its sacramental enactment. Typology, however, does not account in full for the play's characterizations and actions. While Abraham figures God the Father, the patriarch's human limitations are set against the omnipotence and perfection of the Father whose Word he receives and fulfills. The pity and empathy the drama evokes for Abraham would be misplaced if directed toward the deity. But they are quite appropriate emotions for the audience to feel toward the good man who, in his obedience to God, performs unfathomable actions. Evoking sympathy for a priestlike character, the play could effectively undermine contemporary anti-clericalism.

Abraham's opening speech begins with a statement of the efficacy of prayer.

> Adonay, thou god veray,
>> Thou here vs when we to the call,
> As thou art he that best may,
>> Thou are most socoure and help of all.
>
> (1–4)

He prays for mercy, recalls the events the audience has already witnessed, and alludes to others, stressing finally the common end of all humanity.

> . . . adam is to hell gone,
>> And ther has ligen many a day,
> And all oure elders, euerychon,
>> Thay ar gone the same way,
> Vnto god will here thare mone;
>> Now help, lord, adonay!
> ffor, certis, I can no better wone,
>> And ther is none that better may.
>
> (41–48)

God, on high, responds, "I will help adam and his kynde" (49). Thus Abraham's prayer, for the dead "elders" as well as for himself, is proved efficacious, and a special theological emphasis is created. As the late medieval proliferation of obits and chantry foundations testifies, the efficacy for the dead of living worshipers' prayers was an important and much-acted-upon point of doctrine.[19] It was also another point of doctrine to which Lollards objected, thus: "Special preyeris for dede men soulis mad in oure chirch preferryng on þe name more þan anothir, þis is þe false ground of almesse dede, on þe qwiche alle almes houses of Ingelond ben wikkidly igroundid."[20] Although neither Abraham's prayer nor God's response actually "prefers" individuals, what the audience is likely to have focused on is the mention of names in this prayer for the dead. The cycle once again voices through a protopriest an orthodox response to the heretical climate of his day.

That Abraham is a protopriest continues to be significant as the action unfolds. God appears and commands the sacrifice of Isaac; the remainder of the play presents Abraham in a sacerdotal role as he enacts his obedience. Abraham's obedience is signaled by the word "fulfill," a word that reverberates throughout the cycle. First used in God's Creation speech ("that I haue thoght I shall fulfill" [Creation, 17]), it is later repeatedly associated with the Incarnation, the Passion, and the Harrowing of Hell.[21] The cumulative meaning is the complete fulfillment of God's Word, his salvific plan. Thus, when Abraham greets God with, "To here thi will, redy I am, / And to fulfill, whateuer it be" (63–64), he signifies his willingness to participate obediently in the work of salvation, as Abel and Noah before him have done. Deeply engrained typological patterns as well as the drama's design constrain the audience to conflate Abraham's sacrifice with the Eucharistic oblation. Thus, the play reinforces the embattled doctrine that the Mass embodies and fulfills God's Word.

The perversion of the domestic hierarchy has been depicted in the *Mactacio Abel*, and the *Noe* has dramatized the righting of that hierarchy. In the *Abraham*, the patriarch's willing service to his sovereign is reflected in his dependents' service to him: his love for God is matched by Isaac's love, in word and deed, for him. Isaac becomes a model for the devout parishioner whose blind trust in his pastor proves not to be misplaced: "I am redy to do this dede, / And euer to fulfill youre bydyng" (139–40). The use of the connotatively rich "fulfill" both here and in the servant's speech (150) strengthens the suggestion that each parishioner, under clerical guidance, contributes to the fulfillment of the divine Word and its redemptive promise.

As the audience knows well, Abraham will not, ultimately, be required to sacrifice Isaac. Still, the dramatic suspense builds to the point at which God sends an angel to revoke his command.

> say, Isaac shall not be slayn;
> he shall lif, and not be brent.
> My bydyng standis he not agane,
> Go, put hym out of his intent
> Byd hym go home agane,
> I know well how he ment.
>
> (235–40)

The implicit corollary—that those who do stand against God's bidding *may* be burnt—might well have evoked a frisson in this era of *De haeretico comburendo.* Although the play's conclusion is missing from the Towneley manuscript, the probability is that it focused on the substitution of an animal—most likely a sheep or lamb, as in the analogues—for the human sacrifice. The final tableau, grouping priest, parishioner, and agnus, would sharply prefigure the Mass.

Following the *Abraham,* the seventy lines of the fragmentary *Isaac* recount—with minimal drama and invention—the events of Gen. 27:26 to 28:5: Isaac's mistaken blessing of Jacob, Esau's reaction, and Rebekah's decision that Jacob be sent away to evade both Esau's wrath and the dangers represented by the Hittite women. While a two-leaf lacuna in the Towneley manuscript impedes analysis, it remains clear that the play centers on the transmission of God's blessing, another priestly function, by Isaac.

"The later Middle Ages," as Jungmann asserts, "was a thriving era for blessings. All the products of nature and all the objects of human use were recipients of the Church's benedictions."[22] Within the Mass ritual, the priest several times calls down and transmits God's blessing, and the Mass indeed concludes dramatically with such a blessing.[23] The cycle's references to blessing could therefore serve to illuminate the spectators' liturgical experience, bolstering both the priest's importance and the sense that God's Word informed the sacramental ritual. Within the Old Testament sequence, the progression of God's blessing is an important thematic focus. In the *Noe,* God's final words to the patriarch are words of blessing.

> Noe, to the and to thi fry
> My blyssing graunt I;
> Ye shall wax and multiply,
>   And fill the erth agane
> When all thise floodis ar past / and fully gone away.
>
> (*Noe,* 177–81)

God's blessing upon Abraham and his descendents is transmitted by the angel sent to prevent the sacrifice.

> He has persauyd thy mekenes
>   And thi good will also, Iwis;
> he will thou do thi son no distres,
>   ffor he has graunt to the his blys.
>
> (*Abraham,* 265–68)

The *Isaac,* in its turn, is concerned with Isaac's transmission of
the divine blessing to Jacob.

> The blyssing my fader gaf to me,
> god of heuen & I gif the;
> God gif the plente grete,
> of wyne, of oyll, and of whete;
> And graunt thi childre all
> to worship the, both grete and small;
> who so the blyssis, blyssed be he;
> who so the waris, wared be he.
>
> (7–14)

What is curious about this last blessing is its divergence from
the biblical original, particularly in a play of otherwise close
scriptural fidelity. In Gen. 27:28–29, Jacob is blessed with a
promise of "the dew of heaven, / and of the fatness of the earth,"
as well as "plenty of grain and wine" and preeminence among
nations. In the play, it is Esau who receives a leftover blessing of
"the dew of heuen & frute of land" (34). The playwright also
specifies, extrabiblically, that the grain with which Jacob is
blessed is "whete," and he adds "oyll" to the biblical list. The
force of these changes is to differentiate the layperson from the
cleric. Esau, like the lay audience, occupies the natural world.
Jacob, like the priest, ascends to the supernatural in his possession of God's blessing and—implicitly—in his ability to transmit
it, using the sacramental materials of bread and wine.

Jacob's oil comes into play in the succeeding drama, and it too
enhances his priestly characterization. In the *Jacob,* another protochurch is created as the patriarch raises and anoints an altar.

> I promyse to the, with stedfast hart,
> As thou art lord and god myne,
> and I Iacob, thi trew hyne,
> This stone I rayse in syne to day
> shall I hold holy kyrk for ay;
> And of all that newes me
> rightwys tend shall I give the.
>
> (52–58)

Like Abel, Jacob is depicted both as a venerable cleric and, in his
promise to tithe righteously, as a model for all parishioners.

* * *

The two plays that close the Old Testament sequence continue to explore the goodness and power of priesthood, as well as the priest's crucial role in the transmission and fulfillment of God's Word. In the *Pharao*, the wicked ruler's soldiers tell him of the rapid multiplication of the "chyldyr of Israel" (36), and the audience recognizes the fruition of the divine blessing granted to Noah and transmitted down through his lineage. The play's first reference to Moses is deliberately couched to define him as a type of Christ.

> My lord, we haue hard oure faders tell,
> and clerkis that well couth rede,
>   ther shuld a man walk vs amell
> that shuld fordo vs and oure dede.
>
> (67–70)

But like his patriarchal predecessors, Moses is also a protopriest. He enters, thanking God for saving him, in infancy, from Pharaoh's murderous intent, and he tells the audience of his current occupation.

> Now am I sett to kepe,
>   vnder thys montayn syde,
> Byshope Iettyr shepe,
>   to better may be tyde.
>
> (97–100)

Scripturally, Jethro—Moses' father-in-law—is a priest. By elevating him to the episcopate, the playwright permits the spectator to see Moses as the priest: keeping the bishop's sheep is an apt description of the parish priest's commission.

Moses becomes more significantly priestly when God charges him with the deliverance from Pharaoh of the children of Israel. Moses accepts the task of carrying God's Word to Pharaoh, where he will be required to engage in debate with an unbeliever. Pharaoh, interestingly, is not impressed by Moses' "tokyn" (243) of turning his wand into a serpent and back to a wand again. Like many another doubter, Pharaoh is not swayed by phenomena a Lollard would term "false miraclis."[24] Like a staunch heretic, Pharaoh is unmoved by words and miracles, but he is shaken when his life is endangered by the tenth plague, "pestilence" (358), according to the Towneley playwright. Moses is then able to shepherd his flock to the Red Sea and through it, while Pharaoh and his soldiers, praying to "mahowne" (412), are drowned. The identification of the Egyptians as worshipers of "mahowne" enhances the episode's potential counter-Lollard force. Wyclif was called many names by his detractors. He was identified not only with the likes of Satan and Cain, but also, quite specifically, with the founder of Islam. According to William Wolf Capes, "Adam of Usk spoke of [Wyclif] as Mahomet, who preached incontinence to the young and confiscation to the rich."[25]

At the close of the play, Moses offers thanksgiving for yet another salvation "out of the see" (417). The priestly patriarch has administered his people's baptism, and he ends the play with a brief sermon.

> As rayn or dew on erth doys lyght
> And waters herbys and trees full well,
> Gyf louyng to goddys mageste,
>   hys dedys ar done, hys ways are trew,
> honowred be he in trynyte,
>   to hym be honowre and vertew.
>
> (426–31)

The theme of the succeeding *Processus prophetarum* is the transmission of God's Word, by specially selected individuals, through the ages preceding that of the Incarnation. The play's function is to denote the passage of considerable time while demonstrating God's plan, its revelation and fulfillment, as the constant in human experience.[26] The play is incomplete, but its purpose and technique are clearly revealed in the extant fragment. Its speeches shift the cycle's focus away from God's Word as it was spoken to the patriarchs. Yet, as it creates a new focus on the Word Incarnate, the play manifests the identity of Word, Son, and—implicitly—sacrament. Filling the time between Moses and the Incarnation with prophecy, the play condenses the previously established themes of the Word to focus on its once-for-all work of redemption.

The transition from the *Pharao* to the *Prophets* is achieved smoothly through Moses' role in the latter play. E. Catherine Dunn points out that Moses, both at the end of the *Pharao* and at the beginning of the *Prophets,* is addressing an onstage audience of the "folk of Israell."[27] Moses thus brings with him from the earlier play his priestly characterization, and he bestows its aura on the speakers who follow him in the *Prophets.* Already established as one who speaks with God and transmits his Word, Moses speaks immediately of the Word's redemptive fulfillment.

Defining Christ as a prophet, Moses' speech suggests the Incarnation of the Word without detracting from Christ's humanity.

> Therfor will god styr and rayse
> A prophete, in som man dayes,
>   Of oure brethere kyn;
> And all trowes as he says,
> And will walk in his ways,
>   ffrom hell he will theym twyn.

> (7–12)

Moses then turns to a more immediate transmission of God's Word to his audience. "God that has all in wold, / Gretys you bi me" (32–33), he says, introducing his recitation of the Ten Commandments. Robert A. Brawer, using the term "dramatic sermons"[28] to characterize the play's prophecies, points out the playwright's technique for effecting the interpenetration of scriptural and contemporary worlds. Because of the familiar homiletic form, the spectators include themselves with the Israelites as part of Moses' audience. Simultaneously, their awareness of God's Word as the content of all sermons is enhanced and with it their reverence for the clerical transmitter. Moses' speech as a whole prepares the audience for the *Pagina doctorum* in which Jesus' knowledge of the commandments will define him as the Word that was "in the beginning."

David's prophecy, like Moses', reaches both backward and forward in time. Presenting himself as king of Israel, David harks back to the Word that formed and named a nation. Prophesying the advent of the "lord and kyng of all" (127), he describes that Word's future manifestation. When he prophesies the advent of "lyght" (142), David alludes not only to the Nativity but also to humanity's salvation and his own at the Harrowing of Hell. In the Towneley play depicting the latter event, both he and Moses will complete their roles in the cycle as they are led from hell by the Redeemer whose prophets they have been.

The Sibyl announces her prophecy as "tythyngis glad, / of hym that all this warld made" (163–64). Her vision extends from this first historical manifestation of the Word to its last, the Judgment. Reaching out to the end of time, the Sibyl's prophecy extends through the audience's own age to the moment when "all shall see hym with thare ee" (178), and the just and unjust alike will hear the words determining their eternal state. Contrastingly, Daniel's prophecy points to a single moment, that of Christ's birth. Whatever prophecies may have followed Daniel's in the lost portion of the play, his prepares the audience for the thematic focus of the cycle's next eight plays.

*   *   *

   The Old Testament plays of the Towneley cycle recount the history of God's Word from its work of creation to the dawn of the Incarnation. As it was, to the medieval Christian, a constant in human experience, so the Word is a thematic constant unifying the sequence. Typology functions importantly in these plays, pointing ahead to Christ's life and death, the central historical actions in the fulfillment of God's salvific plan. Still more importantly, the playwrights' frequent evocation of the audience's liturgical experience points ahead to the contemporary priest's centrality and the Word's sacramental fulfillment. Focusing on the contemporary Church and identifying Word and sacrament as one, the plays reveal their design. The Towneley Old Testament sequence uses Scripture to combat contemporary heresies, turning against the Lollards the Bible they claimed as their own.

5

The Word Incarnate: Infancy Plays

Throughout the Old Testament sequence, protopriest characters function to transmit God's Word as it evolves toward its Incarnation and subsequent sacramental fulfillment. Foreshadowings of that fulfillment recur frequently in these plays. Because the protopriests are thus associated with sacramental ritual, the plays clearly encourage the audience's allegiance to the orthodox priesthood, not to those clergymen who affiliated themselves with Lollardy. Sacramental reference in the Old Testament plays also serves to reinforce the orthodox notion of God's Word: that is, that the Word reverberates beyond its confinement in scriptural text to reach the worshiper through the liturgy and the sacraments.

Prior to the plays concerning Christ's life and death, the cycle has several times invoked the Eucharist through dramatic language and action. Abel's offering, the Noah family's "feest," Abraham's oblation, and Jacob's blessing all call to the spectators' minds familiar liturgical images. While these plays all contribute to the orthodox sacramental emphasis of the cycle, it is not until the beginning of the New Testament sequence that this technique fulfills its greatest potential as a counterforce against heresy. The embattled doctrine of the Real Presence is powerfully validated in the core of this substantively Corpus Christi play. In their presentation of Christ's life and death, these episodes do not memorialize a historical figure so much as they vivify the sacramentally present Christ whom the spectators know in their own time. In keeping with the Corpus Christi occasion and in opposition to Lollard unbelief, the cycle embodies and intensifies this knowledge. Christ's historical life—what he said and did on earth before his death—is less important to the audience than what he now, "in form of bred," continues to "say" and do. The protopriest figure continues to serve this emphasis, but new techniques also emerge.

The first nine plays of the cycle's central group treat of the events surrounding the Nativity. While God's Word is fulfilled in the Incarnation, the fulfillment is not yet complete, and Christ's birth inevitably evokes an entire sequence of events. That sequence culminates in the Resurrection, and its effect is perpetuated through the sacramental Presence. It is not surprising that the Nativity plays, from within their celebratory context, point ahead to the Passion, death, and Resurrection—and beyond, to the Eucharist.

Theresa Coletti, in an analysis of the N-Town Marian plays, discusses the patristic background to the tradition of interpreting the Nativity in Eucharistic terms.

> From early Christian times the Incarnation had been given Eucharistic interpretations, and patristic writers such as Ambrose, John Chrysostom, and Gregory the Great developed and expanded the sacramental associations of the Nativity. The Eucharistic meanings of the Nativity were strengthened by the etymological interpretation of Bethlehem as the *domus panis*—house of bread—and hence by the analogy between the birth of Christ and the Bread of Life.[1]

The cycle playwrights may well have been directly familiar with patristic tradition, but the generally unlearned audience had other, compelling reasons for making such connections. In the plays of Christ's infancy, two particular strands of devotional tradition intertwine to establish a powerful equation between the infant Jesus and the Eucharist and to continue the previous plays' validation of priesthood. One of these strands, as Leah Sinanoglou has convincingly demonstrated, is that of visions experienced at the elevation of the Host, visions in which "the bread of the Eucharist is transformed between the very hands of the priest at Mass into a small living child, then slain and dismembered before the eyes of the congregation."[2] As Sinanoglou's extensive documentation of the tradition suggests, the medieval Christian is unlikely to have been able to regard an image of the Christ Child without thinking of the adult's sacrificial death and its enactment in the Mass. The reverse is also true: worshipers were encouraged to imagine the appearance of the Child as they gazed at the elevated Host. Sinanoglou demonstrates that the Child-Host conflation underlies the design of the majority of the extant cycles' infancy plays and strikingly enhances their Eucharistic reference.[3]

The second devotional tradition informing the infancy plays is that of the vernacular elevation prayer.[4] In the late fourteenth and

fifteenth centuries, worshipers at Mass were instructed to greet
Christ made present in the elevated Host.

> A litel belle men oyse to ryng.
> þen shal þou do reuerence
> to ihesu crist awen presence,
> þat may lese alle baleful bandes;
> knelande holde vp bothe þi handes,
> And so þo leuacioun þou be-halde,
> for þat is he þat iudas salde,
> and sithen was scourged & don on rode,
> and for mankynde þere shad his blode,
> and dyed & ros & went to heuen,
> and ȝit shal come to deme vs euen.
>
> . . . .
> for-þi I rede with gode entent
> þat þou biholde þis sacrament.
> swilk prayere þen þou make,
> also lykes best þe to take.
> sondry men prayes sere,
> Ilk mon on his best manere.[5]

The greeting prayers taught to parishioners were most frequently
based on a "Hail" or "Welcome" anaphora.[6] It is probable that
spectators of the cycles associated such lyrics exclusively with
the moment of the elevation. In the infancy plays, the characters'
recitation of such prayers functions importantly in the equation
of the Christ Child with the consecrated Host.

Well before the Child appears on the stage, allusions in the
drama evoke this equation. For instance, in the *Caesar Augustus*,
the emperor hears the disquieting prophecy "that in this land
shuld dwell a may, / The which sall bere a chylde, thay say, / That
shall youre force down fell" (70–72). Outraged, the emperor
vows that he will kill the Child as soon as he learns of his birth.
Thus, even before the birth, the infant is imaged in a threatening
situation that will call forth the audience's emotionally charged
association between the Child and the bleeding Host. The emperor's kinsman, Sirinus, also voices murderous intent.

> I counsell you, as ete I brede,
>   what best thereof may be;
> Gar serche youre land in euery stede,
> And byd that boy be done to dede,
>   who the fyrst may hym see.
>
> (182–86)

Although "as ete I brede" is a conventional tag, metrical filler, it is possible that its use here, as in the *Noe* play earlier, projected significant reverberations. The reference to eating bread in Sirinus's speech, occurring in the context of a plan to murder a child, takes on Eucharistic connotations and, ironically, makes of Augustus's kinsman an unwitting spokesman for the sacrament. At the same time, however, as worshipers of "mahowne" (there are references to "mahowne" at lines 9, 122, 127, 147, 151, 162, 208, 226, 238—the dramatist is insistent), these characters are defined as heretics and aligned, at least potentially, with Lollardy.

The *Annunciacio* and *Salutacio* also intervene before the Child appears on the stage. These plays are primarily concerned with the transmission of God's Word to Mary, with Joseph's "trouble" and Elizabeth's contrastingly joyful response to the news of the Incarnation. Ironically, Joseph, while he is still distraught in his ignorance of the true nature of Mary's pregnancy, is the first character in the cycle to refer to Jesus as a "foode" (178).[7] The word is a common synonym for "child" or "youth," but the dramatist may well be using Joseph as the mouthpiece for a connotatively laden sacramental pun.

It is in the ensuing shepherds' plays—both written by the Wakefield Master—that the Child-Host motif emerges in the context of the elevation prayer tradition, and it is in these plays that the protopriest figure returns to the Towneley stage. Like Abel and Moses, the protagonists of these plays are shepherds. They are common people, easy targets of identification for many members of the audience. But they are also potentially clerical pastors, and the plays' actions permit them to fulfill that potential. In both plays, their use of language is an index of their spiritual progress. From "janglyng" and quarreling, they ascend to the priestly functions of retelling prophecy and participating in communion.[8]

The shepherds do indeed complain about many aspects of their earthly existence, but the nature of their dissent must be carefully considered. Rossell Hope Robbins draws a relevant distinction between those dissent-spirited writings that "attack the very heart of the Establishment, the theory of the Three Estates"—many of Wyclif's writings fall into this category—and other complaints: "Squibs and lampoons will bring about no change in the distribution of power, and exposés of such blemishes [personal immoralities] constitute no clear and present danger—and that is why these were tolerated." Robbins indeed cites the Towneley shepherds' complaints as an example of such tolerable dissent.[9] Although they complain about social conditions, these shepherds cannot be mistaken for Lollards.

On the contrary, even at the very outset the shepherds' orthodox priestly potential is recurrently suggested. For instance, Gyb, the Primus Pastor of the first of the two shepherds' plays, bitterly laments his sheep's death of the "rott." Although Gyb is still far from fulfilling his role as a spiritual pastor, the unfolding drama requires the audience to hold it in mind. Gyb's concern for his flock's well-being reflects his capacity for more spiritual pastoral concerns. When the shepherd sets out to "by shepe" (43, 101), similarly, he mirrors the concern of the pastor for his flock's redemption, for Christ "boght" (313) all humankind.

Slow-pace, the third shepherd, also reflects his clerical potential early in the play, albeit in comic-ironic fashion. Slow-pace interrupts the quarrel of his two fellows as he arrives "fro the myln-whele" (126) with a sack of grain, and he points out to the audience the witlessness of the quarrel. He declares Gyb and Horne "bare of wysdom" (161) and comments on their foolishness by enacting a comic parable, spilling his grain to illustrate their absence of "wyttys" (171). However, the comedy is largely at Slow-pace's expense, for he demonstrates that his is the greater foolishness. Although his fellows have nearly come to blows over imaginary sheep, he has wasted real meal to make his point. Horne responds: "May we not be fane! / He has told vs full plane / Wysdom to sup" (176–78). While Horne is expressing his exasperation with Slow-pace's "wisdom," he is also, unknowingly, the mouthpiece for a Eucharistic joke. Christ, scripturally named "Wisdom,"[10] is "supped" in the sacrament. The conventional iconographic depiction of a mill that grinds the "grain" of Old Testament prophecy to produce the "bread" (often portrayed in the form of Eucharistic wafers) of the New Testament may also underlie this episode.[11] Once again, the shepherds' spiritual potential is evoked: they themselves will be prophets later in the play. While this mill iconography may not have been known to the majority of the spectators, the notion of "eating wisdom" remains an accessible Eucharistic allusion. It is significant that the first reference to eating in a play whose first half is dominated by a feast establishes the association between eating and communion.

That feast, although it reveals the shepherds to be as yet inadequate pastors, is itself liturgically evocative. Critical commentary has assessed the meal's significance in several ways. A. C.

Cawley argues that the feast is imaginary; he and William F. Munson share the view that the range of foods described—both peasant and aristocratic fare—is intended comically and points up the feast's literal impossibility.[12] Margery M. Morgan perceives theological meaning in the imaginary feast: the meal is one of several instances of "high fraud" in the Wakefield shepherds' plays, designed to demonstrate that unredeemed humanity's "real" world is an illusion.[13] Alicia K. Nitecki reads the feast as "simultaneously a parody and type of the Eucharist." Nitecki finds numerous specific resonances that connect the feast with the sacramental rite.[14] Lois Roney expands on Nitecki's observations to argue persuasively that "the whole comic interlude of the *First Shepherds Play*, from the imaginary sheep to the distribution of the leftovers, is a parody of the separate incidents and expectations of the sacrament of the Eucharist."[15]

The feast is indeed comic. It is illusory at least in that the shepherds do not recognize its potential significance, and an important part of that significance is Eucharistic. Gyb, for example, begins by suggesting a drink, but Slow-pace would rather eat, for "what is drynk withoute mete?" (194). His question, natural as it is, evokes the dual species of the sacrament, and this allusion is reinforced by his assertion that he is "worthy the wyne" (199). Similarly, words and phrases used to describe the feasting operate on two levels. The feast is itself referred to as a "mangere" (201; also "mangyng" is used for "eating" at 232). The usage is not uncommon, but purposive double entendre operates here. The shepherds at their "mangere" are not yet pastors; they are still sheep in need of their Shepherd. Further, the word refers explicitly to the setting in which that Shepherd will soon be found. Slow-pace fares "full yll" (200) at the "mangere" of his fellows, but he will fare well indeed at the Christ Child's manger—and at the recurrent liturgical feast.[16]

The "feast" begins with Gyb's cry, "Lo, here browne of a bore!" (212). A bizarre collection of viands is contributed by the three shepherds. Cawley suggests that this comic assortment of "high class and low class table delicacies makes a ludicrous gallimaufry that can never have existed" except in the imagination of the playwright. Cawley also points out that the shepherds "myster no sponys" (231) precisely because there is no food.[17] The theological message conveyed is that earthly food is an illusion. As it cannot bring fulfillment of anything but the shepherds' "bellys" (197), it is finally meaningless. The dramatic embodiment of this notion is the mimed feast, and its antithesis—that which en-

duringly fulfills—is implicit. At the feast's conclusion, Gyb pre-
vails upon Horne to offer "good ayll of Hely" (244). In keeping
with the illusory feast, this "ayll" is not ale.[18] Horne apos-
trophizes the bottle: "Be thou wyne, be thou ayll" (256). In so
doing, he not only brings the bottle's contents into question, he
also evokes the Eucharistic wine. Of all beverages, only this can
rightfully be termed "boyte of oure bayll" (247). But although
their communion is typological, and they are unaware of its
significance, the shepherds are seen to grow spiritually in the
course of the feast.

At the close of the feast, the effects of the shepherds' typological communion are evidenced in their newborn charity.
Quarrelsome before, and even during, the feast, they are now in
harmony and ready to manifest their spiritual growth. Gyb turns
his attention to the leftovers: "Then wold I we fest, / This mete
Who shall / into panyere kest" (280–81) that they may "ffor oure
saules" (283) share it with the poor. No longer physical gluttons,
they are now "gluttons"—universalists and spiritual leaders—in
imitation of Christ ("The Son of man came eating and drinking,
and they say, 'Behold a glutton and a drunkard'" [Matt. 11:19]).
After gathering these fragments, they are spiritually fit to be
gathered into the divine charity of which their charity is the
shadow. It is a mere ten lines later that the angel appears to
announce the birth of Christ, inviting the shepherds to share in
the experience of the Nativity.

After the angelic announcement, the shepherds' pastoral potential is fully attained. God's Word has been brought to the
shepherds, and they embrace it by immediately voicing prophecy. Accepting the Word, they become its vehicles, thus re-
capitulating the progressive history of God's Word that the cycle
has been presenting.

> That same childe is he / that prophetys of told,
> Shuld make them fre / that adam had sold.
>
> (332–33)

> Take tent vnto me / this is inrold,
> By the wordys of Isae / a prynce most bold
>   shall he be.
>
> (334–36)

Embracing the Word another way, the shepherds imitate the
angel's song before setting out for Bethlehem to greet their Lord.
The song and the action that follows it are resonant with litur-

gical implications. Priestlike, the shepherds give voice to a "Gloria" just before enacting a symbolic journey, as it were, from Epistle to Gospel side of the stage. From speaking prophecy, they move on to the core of the Mass as, at Bethlehem, they enter into communion with the Word. For the spectators, the appearance of the Child onstage immediately suggests the Host, and the Child-Host motif is enhanced by the emphasis the shepherds place on seeing the Child (369, 440–48), for seeing the elevated Host was the high point of the Mass for most late medieval Christians. Entering the stable, the shepherds greet the Child with a stream of "Hail" lyrics. Not only in general structure, but also in specific verbal echoes, these lyrics reveal themselves as elevation prayers. Gyb begins with these lines:

> hayll, kyng I the call! / hayll, most of myght!
> hayll, the worthyst of all! / hayll, duke! hayll, knyght!
> Of greatt and small / thou art lorde by right;
> hayll, perpetuall! / hayll, faryst wyght!
>
> (458–61)

An elevation prayer surviving in the Vernon manuscript contains a strikingly similar stanza:

> Heil kyng, heil kniht
>   Heil mon of most miht,
>   Prince in þi Trone,
> Heil Duyk, heil Emperour,
> Heil beo þou gouernour
> Of al þis worldus wone.[19]

Each of the shepherds in turn addresses his prayer to the Child. Along with such epithets as "kyng" and "duke," the prayers contain terms of address that draw attention to the Child as a child: "lytyll tyn mop" (467), "lytyll mylk sop" (469), "praty mytyng" (477). Rather than detracting from the evocation of the elevation, however, these phrases contribute forcefully to it. It was at a level of devotion more profound than what is generally reflected in formalized prayer that the elevated Host was a small, exquisite sacrificial Child, the vision of whom might be vouch-safed to the faithful. The tender epithets, like the familiar rustic scene, do not sentimentalize the Nativity; on the contrary, they powerfully enrich the devout spectator's perceptions of the elevation ritual and of the Eucharistic Presence. The shepherds, like ideal parish priests, provide for the spectators a model of worship in which formalized prayer mingles with tender devotion. Gyb's "Amen" (498) and the shepherds' song "To the lawde of this lam" (501) further reinforce both the liturgical meaning of the Nativity and the personal meaning of the Eucharist to the spectator.

After offering gifts—another sacerdotal function—to the Child, the shepherds hear Mary's prayer for their reward. Mary's words also seal the shepherds' pastoral vocation when she urges them to spread the gospel: "Tell furth of this cas" (491).[20] For the spectators, Mary's prayer also reinforces the contemporary liturgical implications of the scene. Her petitions allude to "virtues" commonly attributed to the devout hearing of Mass or, more specifically, to the sight of the Host at the elevation.[21] Participation in the Mass was popularly supposed to ease the difficulties of a journey ("spede your pase" [492]) and to bring the individual "grace at the hour of death"[22] ("graunt you good endyng" [493]). As a result of their communion experience, the shepherds now may be "restorde" (496). Their Eucharistic devotion is the road to their own salvation and a model for the spiritual progress of the spectators.

The *Secunda Pastorum* reinforces the lessons of the first shepherds' play. The overall structure of the two is similar: moving ever closer to God's Word, shepherds become prophets, and prophets become celebrants at Mass. References to eating and drinking, as in the first play, serve to characterize unredeemed humanity's spiritual hunger and to evoke the Eucharist. A significant difference, however, arises from the shepherds' interaction with Mak and Gyll in the play's comic action. There the shepherds are seen to make significant spiritual progress, before the angelic annunciation, as they take on the clerical task of battling thieves with heretical attributes. If, as some scholars have posited, the play is a revision of the *Prima Pastorum*—or indeed if it is an independent play written later—this added dimension might be taken to suggest that the Wakefield Master became increasingly aware of the counter-Lollard potential of the stage for which he wrote.

As in the earlier play, food allusions begin to appear before the shepherds' pastoral potential is realized. Daw, the third shepherd and servant of the other two, reveals the distance they have yet to travel. Like so many servants in the cycle, he is hungry—"A drynk fayn wold I haue / and somwhat to dyne" (146)—and he complains that his masters do not feed him properly. Both in its evocation of the dual species and in its reference to master feeding servant, Daw's speech emits Eucharistic connotations. Both he and his masters need the remedy they will find in the stable at Bethlehem, the remedy the spectators find in the Mass. Just as Christ is born into the shepherds' historical world, so is he recurrently born in the rite calling forth his Presence.

But a major obstacle blocks the shepherds' path toward redemption. Mak intrudes into their world, claiming—in a southern accent—to be a "yoman . . . of the king" (201). For the northern audience, southerners might evoke immediate distrust, not only because of conventional prejudices but also because of the southerly provenance of heretical thought. The first shepherd's response—"take outt that sothren tothe, / and sett in a torde!" (215–16)—betrays no love for either southerners or Mak. It immediately emerges that Mak is not a southerner, but he does merit distrust.

No shepherd but rather a thief, Mak aligns himself with heresy. He casts a spell to make the shepherds sleep deeply so that he may steal one of their sheep. The association of Mak with sorcery coincides with their detractors' accusations that the Lollards practiced black magic.[23] After a sheep is discovered to be missing, Mak immediately falls under suspicion. The third shepherd says of Mak, "Me thoght he was lapt / in a wolfe skyn"; and the first responds, "So are many hapt / now namely within" (368–69). The notion that the Lollards were wolves "within" was a commonplace in anti-Lollard writings. Archbishop Courtenay referred to the "poor priests," in particular, as wolves in sheep's clothing.[24] Owst cites the diatribe of an orthodox homilist against Lollard preachers. That homilist uses the phrases "feyned holiness" and "shepes clothynge" to describe the heretics, while he refers to their potential converts as sheep. The Lollard, he asserts,

is aferd to openli come among stedfast men in bileve, and therfore he awaiteth whan men berken nouʒt aʒens synne and false techyng, but slepen in synful lustis of flesshe. . . . Also the wolf in kynde is buystouse and stif in bodi; and so an heretik is strong and stif in falshed, . . . hasti in techyng. . . . With her tunge thei magnifien Cristis martiris, but thei wolen not have her pacience. And so speciali ʒe shuln knowe hem bi her unstedfastnesse, and unpacience in adversite. . . . Anoon as ony thyng fallith to hem to worldli welthe, thei waxen proude, and thei ben travelid with boost and with veyn glorie. Thei ben hogeli angwisshid in adversite, and unmesurabli ioyful in prosperite.[25]

This description of the temperamental and lupine Lollard fits Mak exquisitely. Friar Daw Topias voices a similar view in his reply to Jack Upland.

> But, Iack, amonge oure chateryng ȝit wolde I wite
> Whi þat þe lollardis weren moost greye cloþis.
> I trowe to shew þe colour þat signifieþ symplenesse,
> And wiþinne, seiþ Crist, ȝe ben rauenous wolues.[26]

Once Mak reaches home, the play's motif of food and eating is connected with the stolen sheep, and Eucharistic connotations become more obvious and more outrageous. Of the sheep Mak says, "I wold he were slayn / I lyst well ete" (323); the audience thinks of Christ and the Passion he endured in order that they might eat the Eucharistic "Lamb." Gyll offers her counsel that they put the sheep in the cradle and pretend it is a child. The parodic Nativity scene, upon which so much useful commentary has been written, is underway.[27] The sheep/child conflation is amusingly sustained when Mak returns to the shepherds to re-count his dream of the birth of a son "to mend oure flok" (388). The phrase connotes redemption as well as literally referring to Mak's improved livestock holdings; it also enhances the image of Mak as a rival spiritual leader.

The shepherds agree that they must take action to redeem their lost sheep. The third shepherd asserts, "Shall I neuer ete brede / the sothe to I wytt," and the first adds, "Nor drynk in my heede / with hym tyll I mete" (468–69). Once again, the conventional asseveration, "Shall I neuer ete brede," becomes a Eucharistic reference. The "sothe" the shepherds are determined to reach transcends the resolution of the theft; it is, finally, the Truth they will meet in the Bethlehem stable. They will neither eat bread nor drink, spiritually, until they meet "with hym." The antecedent, although the shepherds cannot yet know this, is not Mak but the Christ Child. But the shepherds do know enough to reject the offer of food Mak makes in his attempt to conciliate them: "Nay, nawther mendys oure mode / drynke nor mette" (504). They are waiting for the communion in which they will partici-pate in the play's final scene.

The true meal remains focal as Mak and Gyll colorfully protest their innocence to the shepherds. Pointing to the cradle, Mak says, "As I am true and lele / to god here I pray, / That this be the fyrst mele / That I shall ete this day" (521–22). Gyll, similarly, asserts that if she has ever deceived the shepherds, she will "ete

this chylde / That lygys in this credyll" (537–38). These references forcefully increase the probability that audience members
identified the couple as heretics. The audience hears Eucharistic
reference, yet Mak and Gyll talk as if eating the "Lamb" were a
normal gastronomic experience. The thief and his wife sound
very much like such Lollards as Sir Lawrence St. Martin, who
"when handed the consecrated wafer rose from his knees, took it
home with him, broke it into three pieces and ate one with
oysters, one with onions and one with wine, to show that it was
no different from ordinary bread."[28] But for all their wickedness,
Mak and Gyll ultimately serve the truth. As Sinanoglou states,
Gyll's oath

> is fulfilled, but in a wonderfully unexpected manner. Since she lies, a
> child will be eaten, but not the counterfeit child in her cradle. Rather
> her vow anticipates the birth of the Child of God, born that his folk
> "fully may fede." By referring ostensibly to one child but actually to
> another, Gyll's oath unites two parallel episodes and firmly subordi-
> nates the secular pseudo-nativity to the sacred Nativity which fulfills
> and transcends it.[29]

The shepherds discover and redeem their sheep; they punish a
heretic, but with charitably muted severity. Thus, they make
significant spiritual progress within the first part of the play,
triumphing over the immediate evil Mak represents. The angel's
message, then, comes in some sense as a reward to individuals
who have already begun to function as active Christians. In other
respects, the shepherds of the second play share the experiences
of their predecessors. They too become prophets upon receiving
God's Word from the angelic messenger. They too look forward
specifically to the *sight* of the Child: "fful glad may we be / and
abyde that day / that lufly to se / that all myghtys may" (683–84).
To this, moreover, they add the yearning anticipation of their
prayer to the Child: "lord well were me / for ones and for ay, /
Myght I knele on my kne / some word for to say / To that chylde"
(685–87). The Nativity scene itself is parallel to its counterpart:
the moment is simply recreated for its importance to the Corpus
Christi theme and its powerful immediacy to the audience.
Again, the sight of the Child is stressed; again, the shepherds
enact the Mass and recite elevation prayers. Gyb's "hayll, suf-
feran sauyoure! / ffor thou has vs soght: / hayll, frely foyde and
floure / that all thyng has wroght!" (719–20) parallels the Vernon
manuscript prayer's "Heil fruit, heil flour, / Heil be þou Saueour."
The shepherds mix epithets of awe and tenderness in their

prayers, and they sing as they leave the stable. While the Towneley manuscript does not indicate the nature of their song, it is
likely that it shared the liturgical character and Eucharistic over-
tones of the *Prima Pastorum* song.

The succeeding *Oblacio magorum* reiterates the themes of the
shepherds' plays. Herod, whose raging dramatic persona retained notoriety into Shakespeare's age, now appears on the
stage. He serves two important functions, one of which is to
present a continuing threat to the Christ Child. Not only is
dramatic tension thereby created, but the audience also sustains
a focus on the sacrificial Child, the Child-Host conflation. Herod
is also important in reinforcing the audience's equation of evil
with heresy. The technique is the same as that used in the case of
Pharaoh: worshiping "Mahowne" (27) and enforcing that worship upon others, Herod is presented as a sower of heresy—in the
audience's most immediate and likely interpretation, a Lollard.

The spectators, having experienced their own close kinship
with the shepherds of the previous plays, need feel no distance
from the Christ Child when he appears in this drama. The three
kings' repeated use of the word "worship" (230, 236, 243, 251)
signals not only their humility before Christ, but also their connection with the spectators. Priestlike they are, but not aloof regal
powers: they merit reverence as spiritual leaders, not earthly
rulers. The Nativity is depicted with simplicity and economy;
the kings' "Hail" anaphora once again recalls to the audience
their own participation in the liturgical moment of the elevation.

> hayll be thou, maker of all kyn thyng!
> That boytt of all oure bayll may bryng!
>
> (541–42)

> hayll, ouercomer of kyng and of knyght!
> That fourmed fysh, and fowyll in flyght!
>
> (547–48)

> hayll, kyng in kyth, cowrand on kne!
> hayll, oone-fold god in persons thre!
>
> (553–54)

Social and historical distances dissolve: the kings become the
spectators' pastors as they too are recognized as officiants at
Mass.

This pattern for the depiction of the Christ Child is interrupted
briefly by his appearance in the *Fugacio in egiptum*. The play

does not, however, detract from the cycle's emphasis on the sacramental Christ; rather, it tonally qualifies that emphasis. While the earlier plays stress the joy the Eucharist brings to the Christian—the focus, to be sure, of the Corpus Christi feast[30]— the *Fugacio* reminds the audience of the sorrow at the core of that joy. The Christ Child's existence in the sacrifice of the Mass is here presented to them not through direct liturgical associations; rather, as in the opening of the *Oblacio magorum*, by the depiction of the Child in a threatening situation. Because the brief action centers on the threat against the Child's life, the entire play serves to anticipate the Passion and death of Christ. The audience is reminded of that death's inevitability. Prepared by the focus of the preceding plays, they also see beyond it to the sacrament in which it is commemorated, and through which its efficacy reaches them.

An angel tells Joseph of the danger presented by Herod's murderous plan, and Joseph relays this information to Mary. Mary's role, for which there is no scriptural basis, is determined by the tradition of the Seven Sorrows of Mary. Among the "official" Sorrows, which include Mary's meeting with her son on the road to Calvary and the Crucifixion itself, is the Flight into Egypt.[31] The play's evocation of the Passion is thus both traditional and contributory to the Corpus Christi cycle's design. That evocation is achieved primarily through Mary's speeches, which take the form of brief *Planctus Mariae*. Theologically "incorrect" but devotionally exemplary, these speeches anticipate Mary's sorrow at the death of her son.

> Alas! I lurk and dare!
> To slo this barne I bare,
> > what wight in warld had wyll?
> his hart shuld be full sare
> Sichon for to fare
> > That neuer yit dyd yll,
> > Ne thought.
>
> > > > > (83–89)

> his ded wold I not se,
> > ffor all this warld to wyn;
> Alas! full wo were me,
> > In two if we shuld twyn;
> My chyld so bright of ble.
> To slo hym were pyte,
> > And a full hedus syn.
>
> > > > > (105–11)

> Alas, full wo is me!
>   Is none so wyll as I!
> My hart wold breke in thre,
> My son to se hym dy.

(157—60)

Mary's acute grief draws the spectator's own devotional response: the invitation to such emotional extremes was surely one of the attractions of late medieval orthodox religion, and it was the antithesis of the sort of spiritual experience sought by Lollardy. That the Eucharist shimmers beyond the Passion cannot be forgotten. Mary's tripartite heartbreak evokes the fraction of the Host. As the play draws to a close, Joseph reassures the lamenting Mary that by flight they may "saue thi foode so fre" (164); the audience's attention is focused upon the sacramental "food" that continues to sustain them.

The Christ Child does not appear in the succeeding *Magnus Herodes*, although the theme of the *Fugacio* is sustained in the murder of children who are surrogates for the Child. It is also noteworthy that this play's author, the Wakefield Master, borrows a device he found in the cycle as it came to his hands. Like the earlier author(s) of the *Pharao*, the *Caesar Augustus*, and the *Oblacio magorum*, the Wakefield Master characterizes evil specifically in terms of the worship of "mahowne," suggesting heresy in general, and, in particular, the chroniclers' alias for Wyclif himself. Indeed the play opens with an invocation to "Most myghty mahowne," and other references to the "false god" abound (10, 54, 127, 429, 458, 459, 473). In the play, Herod quickly works himself up into one of his characteristic rages, and another dimension is added to the king's heretical character. Having heard vague prophecies of Christ's Advent, Herod demands more information of his counselors, but he very specifically limits the sources they may consult.

> Syrs, I pray you inquere / in all wrytyng,
> In vyrgyll, in homere / And all other thyng
>   Bot legende;
> Sekys poece tayllys;
> lefe pystyls and grales;
> Mes, matyns, noght avalys,
>   All these I defende.

(201—7)

Herod purports to be seeking the Word, the truth of prophecy, but
not only is he characterized as a pagan who would look for truth
only in such writers as Virgil and Homer; he also pointedly—and
anachronistically—refuses to look for it in "legende" (saints'
lives or a liturgical lesson book), in any other liturgical service
books, or in the services themselves. The force of the anachronism could function to align Herod still more closely with the
cycle's other Lollard-like heretics. Like Wyclif himself, Herod
discounts exactly those repositories of truth that the orthodox
Church held to be as central as the Bible.[32]

In the *Purificacio Marie*, the Christ Child reappears, and the
evocation of the audience's liturgical experience achieves a new
prominence. While the earlier plays have clearly suggested the
setting, actors, and actions of the Mass, the *Purificacio* goes
beyond suggestion: it has an actual liturgical setting, the temple,
Symeon's "kyrk" (42). The play begins with Symeon's monologue, in which he laments his age and infirmity and prays that
he may live long enough to see and touch the prophesied Mes-
siah. An angel appears and tells the old man that his desire will
be fulfilled. A second angel brings "tythyngys of solace" (80):
Symeon is to go at once to the temple, where he will meet the
Child.

With the mention of the temple, the scene becomes increasingly liturgical in contemporary medieval terms. First,
Symeon reemphasizes his desire to see the Child: "Well is me
that I shall dre / Tyll I haue sene hym with myn ee" (88–89); and
the audience recalls the visual communion of the shepherds'
plays. The evocation of the Mass is enhanced by the inclusion of
two details unique to the Towneley version of the episode: Symeon puts on a "vestment" (95), and bells spontaneously ring. A
bell was rung immediately prior to the elevation as well as at
other times during the liturgical day;[33] that it is the "sakerynge
bell" Symeon hears is suggested by the fact that its ringing
immediately precedes the appearance of Christ in the protochurch. It is worth noting that among the more unusual "errors" to which some Lollards confessed was their antipathy to
church bells, which they described as "Antecristis hornes" or
mere means "to gete mony into prestes purses."[34] Such an attitude seems an ironic tribute to the power of the liturgical scene
here evoked.

According to the extant fragment of stage direction, angels
begin to sing at Mary and Joseph's entrance, with the Child, into

the temple; the liturgical atmosphere is further heightened. Staging may have reinforced the sacramental reference of the scene. It is possible that Symeon took the Child in his arms and elevated him above the altar. The play as we have it ends with additional emphasis, in an angel's speech, on the sight of the Child.

> Thou, symeon, rightwys and trew,
> Thou has desyred both old and new,
> To haue a sight of cryst ihesu
>   As prophecy has told!
> Oft has thou prayd to haue a sight
> Of hym that in a madyn light;
> here is that chyld of mekyll myght.
>   Now has thou that thou wold.
>
>   (133–40)

It is not unlikely that the conclusion of the play, missing from the Towneley manuscript, depicted Symeon's addressing an elevation prayer to the Child, as he does, for example, in the York analogue.

At the conclusion of the infancy plays, the Towneley spectators have been as deeply drawn into the scriptural moment as into the sacramental mystery, for, the cycle proclaims, these are one and the same. Before Christ is ever given a word to say on the Towneley stage, he is pronounced the sacramental Word in nine plays. The cycle transmutes Scripture: this epiphany would not be granted through lay interpretation of the vernacular Bible alone, the spiritual path recommended by the Lollards. Only through the liturgy, only with the guidance of true pastors, can the audience achieve communion with that Word: this, in the Towneley dramatic presentation, is the real Christmas story.

6

The Word Incarnate: Teachings and Sacrifice

The series of plays that follows the infancy sequence relates selected events of Christ's life briefly and, at greater length, dramatizes the Passion. The treatment of the ministry is minimal: indeed, we are given only three glimpses of Jesus between the infancy and the Last Supper. We see him as a child taking on the "doctors" in the temple; we witness his baptism and the raising of Lazarus. Like the anti-Lollard *Mirrour of the blessyd lyf of Jesu Christ*, the drama deals almost perfunctorily with the ministry. Rather than presenting Jesus as a teacher, an admittedly undramatic subject, and calling for an intellectual response to the acts of his earthly life, the playwrights concentrate instead upon the devotion-inspiring Passion. They lead up to that sacrificial core of the drama with incidents economically selected to aid the audience in identifying the Passion with the Mass.

The *Pagina doctorum* encapsulizes the larger drama's progression from the Old Testament to the New, from the Epistle to the Gospel side of the altar. As in the preceding *Purificacio*, Christ's presence in a liturgical setting is focal. Here, the Child, who has been repeatedly equated with the consecrated Host, has his first speaking role, and what he says elaborates the meaning of the sacrament. Although the recitation of the Decalogue is a set piece of didacticism, its function in the play goes beyond this level of significance. By reciting the Ten Commandments and by revealing their spiritual essence—love for God and for one's fellows—Christ demonstrates his role in the fulfillment of the Old Law. More accessible to the audience than the historical Christ is the sacrament in which the ideas of love and fulfillment are embodied. According to John Mirk, in a sermon for the Feast of Corpus Christi, the sacrament exists for four "skylles," one of which is "for gret loue schowing":[1] the Eucharist is a reminder of the love God shows to humanity and the love and charity he asks

of his creatures. The sacrament is itself the clearest sign of the
fulfillment of the Old Law, as the sequence for Mass on the Feast
of Corpus Christi explicitly states.

> On this table of the king,
> our new Paschal offering
>   brings to end the olden rite.
> Here for empty shadows fled
> is reality instead;
>   here, instead of darkness, light.[2]

As in the preceding play, staging may have further enhanced the
Eucharistic reference of this play's action. If the actor portraying
Christ stood upon the altar of the temple—a logical vantage point
for a child addressing adults—he would readily have been seen
as the Real Presence made visible, expounding his own meaning
to doctors and audience alike.

The remainder of the play concerns Mary and Joseph and their
search for their missing son. The loss of her son in the temple is
another of the Seven Sorrows of Mary,[3] and Mary's opening lines
are again a *Planctus*.

> A, dere Ioseph! what is youre red?
>   Of oure greatt bayll no boytt may be;
> My hart is heuy as any lede,
>   My semely son to I hym se.
> Now haue we soght in euery sted,
>   Both vp and downe, thise dayes thre;
> And wheder he be whik or dede
>   yit wote we not; so wo is me!

(193–200)

Mary's lamentation anticipates the Passion and death; Christ's
three days' absence, a scriptural detail, suggests the three days'
entombment. The parents' finding of their son thus foreshadows
his post-Resurrection appearances, both biblical and sacramental. The sacramental suggestion is underlined by Mary and
Joseph's emphasis on the sight of the Child in the temple.

> A, certys, I se that we have soght!
>   In warld was neuer so semely a sight.

(207–8)

> Now sothly, son, the sight of the
> has comforthed vs of all oure care.

(253–54)

The experience of Joseph and Mary in finding their son is not merely a historical fact; it transcends history to become a model for the spectator, for whom the "sight" of Christ in the "temple" will also provide comfort for all care.

In the *Iohannes baptista*, Christ once again appears in a liturgical setting. In this case, however, the setting's liturgical character is defined not by a physical building or altar, but by Christ's presence and by the sacramental action in which he and John participate. John is standing on the bank of the Jordan when two angels appear and tell him he is to baptize Christ. Offering to set off to meet him, John is told that he must await Christ's coming. John draws a general conclusion:

> By this I may well vnderstand
>> That childer shuld be broght to kyrk,
> ffor to be baptysyd in euery land;
>> To me this law yit is it myrk.

> (85–86)

Although there is "no kyrk, ne no bygyng" (91), the riverbank—like the stable in the Nativity scenes—will be seen as a liturgical setting at Christ's entrance. As in the Mass, the Real Presence will hallow the physical environment.

John's opening speech prepares the audience for Christ's entrance. John refers to himself as the "forgangere" (28) who announces the Advent of Christ and prophesies his redemptive death. After describing the Passion, John summarizes: "Thus shall he dy, that frely foode, / And ryse agane tyll oure relefe" (39–40). The use of "foode" in this context strongly suggests the sacramental food that will come to humanity after—and as a result of—Christ's death and Resurrection. The sacramentally connotative "foode" is repeated at line 56: John offers thanks to the Lord, who "ffeydys vs with foode both euen and none."

Christ appears, and the sacraments are directly mentioned for the first time in the cycle. Although the action centers on baptism, John reminds the audience that there are "sex othere" (197) sacraments sent by Christ to his people. This reminder takes on some urgency in the context of Lollard antisacramentalism, which did not limit itself to attacks on the Eucharist alone.[4] And while Lollards at various times taught against all the sacraments, baptism was second only to the Eucharist in the amount of attention it received. Some Lollards affirmed that "baptism could be done as well in a ditch as in a font."[5] In East Anglia, Lollards went so far as to hold "that a child was sufficiently baptized by Christ's passion without any ceremony in church, and that this took place when body and soul were united in the mother's womb."[6]

Baptism merits the playwrights' special attention in part because it was under seige, but also because of its relationship to the Eucharist itself. As Saint Thomas Aquinas wrote, the sacraments "sanctify us and prepare us to receive the Eucharist or to consecrate it. Baptism is required in order to begin this spiritual life; the Eucharist is necessary in order to bring it to its culmination."[7] Direct Eucharistic allusions recur in John's reverence for Christ's "blyssyd body" (135), the angel's reference to Christ as "that frely foode" (164), and John's thankfulness for the "sight" of Christ (207). The play's most striking evocation of the Eucharist is Christ's presentation to John of a lamb.

> This beest, Iohn, thou bere with the,
>   It is a beest full blyst;
>   *hic tradat ei agnum dei*
>   [here he hands him the Lamb of God]
> Iohn, it is the lamb of me,
>   Beest none othere ist;
> It may were the from aduersyte,
>   And so looke that thou tryst;
> By this beest knowen shall thou be,
>   That thou art Iohn baptyst.
>
>   (209–16)

This action, unique to the Towneley baptism play, functions on at least two levels of significance. Rosemary Woolf suggests that it is a sort of dramatized etiological myth, "presumably invented to account for iconographic representations in which John the Baptist is shown holding a lamb, as his emblem."[8] Further, the paschal lamb is a familiar type of the Eucharist; the "lamb of me" in this scene is the figure's fulfillment. The scene is thus a dramatic metaphor for Eucharistic communion. Like the communion of the spectators' experience, John's protocommunion will defend him against "aduersyte," as they and he are exhorted to believe.[9] The "lam" to whom the shepherds of the *Prima Pastorum* sing praise here becomes still more explicitly equated with the consecrated Host. To reinforce the sacramental significance of the interaction between Christ and John, the playwright has John take leave of his Lord with a remarkable punning reference to his sacramental form: "ffarwell! the luflyst that euer was bred!" (263).

The play following the *Iohannes baptista* in the Towneley manuscript is the *Conspiracio;* but the manuscript also contains, after the *Iudicium,* a play of *Lazarus* that, if it was part of the cycle, would presumably have been presented between the play of John the Baptist and those of the Passion sequence.[10] Even aside from its peculiar placement in the manuscript, there is reason to suspect that the *Lazarus* was not part of the Corpus Christi cycle, but rather an independent dramatic piece. More than half of the play is taken up with Lazarus's blood-chilling sermon on the horrors of death and the urgent need for repentance; its tone is far removed from that of the joyful Corpus Christi celebration. Further, the *Lazarus* is the sole play in the manuscript concerning the events of Christ's ministry. The other extant cycles, in addition to the raising of Lazarus, depict the episodes of the woman taken in adultery, Jesus' healing the infirm, Mary Magdalen's anointing of her Lord's feet, and the entry into Jerusalem. The Towneley cycle, contrastingly, places no emphasis on the events of Jesus' ministry: his life is depicted only as a prelude to his death, Resurrection, and sacramental return. Thus, the cycle might have been played devoid of ministry plays without resultant damage to its thematic structure.

The possibility cannot be discounted, however, that the *Lazarus* was part of the cycle, and in that case it need not have detracted from the drama's sacramental focus. The play strikingly demonstrates the power of Christ's Word: "Com furth, lazare, and stand vs by" (97), he says, and a dead man rises from the tomb. The Word spoken to Lazarus is identical with the Word informing the Eucharist, and it is analogous in function: both bring life to the dead, although it is physical life in Lazarus's case and spiritual life for the communicant. The resurrection of Lazarus, after his three days' burial, also directly anticipates Jesus' own Resurrection. If the *Lazarus* was played within the cycle, its most important function was its corrective placement before the Passion plays. Before being drawn into that sequence of absorbing and horrifying events, the audience is reminded that Christ's suffering and death forerun a still more significant event in salvific history: the Resurrection shadowed forth in Lazarus's rise.

*   *   *

With the *Conspiracio* the Passion sequence begins. These plays are, of all the cycle, arguably the most directly and obviously

Eucharistic in reference, the strongest exhortation to faith in the Real Presence. The Mass was, of course, commonly understood to be a reenactment of the Passion, or, more precisely, a continuing enactment of an eternally present event.[11] The most overtly anti-Lollard drama extant, the Croxton *Play of the Sacrament*, achieves its powerful effect by conflating the Passion and the Mass, showing that what is done to the Host was—and perennially is—done to Christ. Just so, the Towneley Passion sequence vivifies the liturgy for the spectators, offering them a visible correlative for the Real Presence and attracting to the sacrament both faith and devotion. It must be conceded that these plays show less emphasis than their predecessors on the portrayal of Lollard-like characters: the Passion sequence's opponents of the word, Steven's "tyrants," have some heretical characteristics, and a sensitized medieval spectator would not have missed them. But this same spectator would have been swept much more forcefully into the pro-orthodoxy of this portion of the cycle—its enactment of the sacrifice that they know best in sacramental terms. It is predominantly positive rather than negative counter-Lollardy that the Passion sequence could effect.

The *Conspiracio* exhibits a tripartite structure: the quiet and moving scene of the Last Supper is sandwiched between dissonant, violent scenes of conspiracy and capture. The structure of the play establishes a pattern for the sequence as a whole: in each play Jesus is central—as on the altar—quiet, inexorable, and surrounded by raucous, violent action. Jesus has very few lines: the Word in these plays is nearly as silent, yet fully as effectual, as it is in the form of the consecrated Host.

The play opens with Pilate's long, ranting speech identifying the speaker as an enemy of God's Word. Pilate is devoted to deceit and hypocrisy; he praises "fals indytars" (24) and "fals out rydars" (26). Serving and served by falsehood, Pilate identifies Christ as the fearful force of truth: "If this be true in deyd, / his shech shall spring and sprede, / And ouer com euer ylkone" (51–53). Caiaphas and Annas enter seeking Pilate's counsel, for the power of their laws is threatened by Jesus' teaching. Identifying themselves with the law and Jesus with "lesyns" (67), these priests delineate their topsy-turvy moral universe. Their law, albeit scriptural, is not finally divine law, for they hope to direct its lethal letter against the Word Incarnate. To be biblically literalist is, potentially, to be anti-Christ: this dramatized message carries counter-Lollard force.

The two priests are not protopriests like Abel or Noah, but first-century Jews. This distinction is important. Because the cycle has presented the Old Testament patriarchs as priestlike in contemporary terms, it is unlikely that the audience will equate Caiaphas and Annas with their own priesthood. Costuming is likely to have sharpened the distinction: Meg Twycross's remarks about the N-Town Passion play are relevant here. When that play's author "gives instructions that his Annas is to be dressed *after a busshop of þe hoold lawe*, he means precisely that: a Jewish High Priest, after the specifications in Exodus 28. The blue tabard is a version of the ephod, and the mitre, as he says, is not a modern one, but the High Priest's tiara. . . . [W]e should realize that because Annas and Caiaphas are called 'bishops', that does not imply that they are contemporary English bishops."[12]

DeWelles argues that the dramatists portray Christ himself in the Passion sequence as Lollard-like in order to criticize clerical overzealousness—personified in the two priests—in seeking out and persecuting Lollards.[13] However, a silent Christ can hardly be Lollard-like: Kendall describes the extraordinary emphasis found in Lollard writings on how the Lollard accused of heresy can best "parry the questions of the bishops and their circle."[14] Despite the charge of heresy flung at Jesus, it is Caiaphas and Annas who are placed in the line of direct descent from the cycle's other heretics, and they are sharply differentiated by their bluster and hostility from the cycle's protopriests. As DeWelles himself asserts, "the linguistic crimes Christ is alleged to have committed—talking too much and cleverly manipulating words—are the very ones his accusers are most guilty of."[15]

Caiaphas and Annas present the evidence against Jesus: he has healed the infirm and preached in contradiction to the law. Pilate's rage grows and culminates, at the mention of Jesus' claim to be "heuens kyng" (121), in a vengeful threat: "By mahowns blood, that shall he aby / with bytter baylls or I ett bred!" (124–25). Once again, the invocation of "mahowne" raises Wyclif's specter. The conventional phrase, "or I ett bred," recurring in the context of an unwitting allusion to the redemptive Passion, evokes the sacrament and reminds the spectators of the enduring and personally relevant significance of the events they are witnessing.

Like the two priests, Judas is a "fals indytar" after Pilate's own heart. The treacherous disciple enhances his credibility with the conspirators by voicing his own complaint about Jesus' "bowrdyng" (228), and he recounts the story of the woman's pouring precious ointment upon Jesus. Judas objects to this, as it seems to him, empty ritual, arguing that the ointment might have been sold to provide means for the poor, not to mention enrichment for Judas himself. Judas's antiritualistic stance may well have resonated, to the contemporary audience, with current heresy. On the stage, a bargain is quickly struck. Pilate praises Judas's decision to sell his Lord: "Now for certan, sir, thou says right wele" (282). The disciple promises to match his words with deeds—"All that I haue here hight / I shall fulfill in dede" (290–91)—but the audience knows that Judas's words prove true and efficacious not because his heretical stance is valid, but because his actions match the divine plan.

Next ensues the Last Supper scene, a scene chiefly notable for what it lacks: a depiction of the Eucharist's institution. This lack and its significance to the cycle's design and purposes will be fully discussed in chapter 7. Of the scene itself, what is most striking is its quiet dignity and the contrast it presents with what precedes and follows it. Although the suspense of the unfolding conspiracy is maintained in the dramatic revelation of Judas's treachery, what dominates the scene is a strong sense of Jesus' knowledge of and cooperation in an inevitable plan. Although cast as the victim in Pilate's scenario, Jesus is in control of himself and, finally, of the action. As the orthodox Church will endure despite heretical upheavals, so Jesus will endure, triumphing over ephemera.

The foot-washing episode makes clear that Christ will live on in those who follow his example.

> Now wote ye what I haue done;
>   Ensampyll haue I gyffen you to;
> loke ye do eft sone;
>   Ichon of you wesh othere fete, Lo!
>
> (408–11)

He will endure, too, in the Presence he will manifest after he has gone to his "fader house" (436).

> I shall com to you agane,
>   and take you to me,
> That where so euer I am,
>   ye shall be with me.
>
> (444–47)

I shall com eft to you agayn:
　　this warld shall me not se,
Bot ye shall se me well certan,
　　and lyfand shall I be.

(456–59)

He alludes both to his post-Resurrection appearances and to his Presence in the Eucharistic sacrament. The sacrament celebrated by the cycle as a whole remains focal as Christ's earthly life nears its terrible end. The inevitability and divine causality of the unfolding action are stressed in Jesus' prayer and the answer it receives. A model of perfect obedience to God's Word, Jesus awaits his capture knowing it to be necessary to the redemptive plan.

The stage is now invaded by Pilate, violently crying "Peas!" (560), with Judas and the soldiers. The soldiers boast of the valiant deeds they will accomplish: "as euer ete I breede" (622), one claims, he will kill Christ; another asserts that the soldiers would not fear to "bynde the dwill" (633) if the need arose. In their very opposition to Jesus, these men speak words that evoke his triumph over evil, at the Harrowing of Hell, and his sacramental endurance. But knowing not what they speak, the soldiers are "janglyng," and their abuse of language provides a sharp contrast to Jesus' calm preparations for his capture. Speaking to Peter of Judas as one who "bryngys up slaunder" (656), Jesus emphasizes that the traitor's act springs from his enmity to the Word. When Jesus is taken and brought before Pilate, he remains silent while his adversaries bicker about his fate. It is this silence on the part of the Word Incarnate that, paradoxically, dominates the remaining plays of the Passion sequence.[16] Jeffrey Helterman's incisive discussion stresses that Jesus' silence proclaims him as the Word whose "presence is itself the message He brings."[17] The Word's truth need not be voiced; it is indeed most effectively conveyed in the silent sacramental Presence.

In the *Coliphizacio*, a Wakefield Master play, Jesus' almost complete silence continues to contrast sharply with the "janglyng" of his tormentors and inquisitors. At the play's opening, the Tortores assure the captive source of all grace that he will get "no grace" (3) from the high priests. Ironies multiply as the Tortores chatter slanderously about Jesus' alleged abuses.

　　[*Primus tortor.*] ffare wordys can thou paynt / and lege lawes new.
　　Secundus tortor. Now be ye at003 / for we will persew
　　　　On this mater.

Many wordys has thou saide
Of which we ar not well payde;
As good that thou had
   halden still thi clater.

(21—27)

Approaching the high priests, the Primus Tortor plans to "tell of
his talkyng" (45). Leading in the pointedly silent Jesus, the tormentors repeat their accusations before Caiaphas and Annas.

He has bene for to preche / full many long yeris;
And the people he teche / a new law.

(65—66)

He lyes for the quetstone.

(80)

He wold fayne downe bryng / oure lawes bi his steuen.

(92)

From the spectators' viewpoint, however, the Tortores' very accusations express tribute to the power of the Word.
   Having been inundated with complaints about Jesus'
"wordys," Caiaphas is eager to hear the prophet speak. The
priest's methods are puerile: he fires off repeated insults in the
attempt to shock or anger Jesus into involuntary response.

Illa-hayll was thou borne! / harke! says he oght agane?
Thou shall onys or to-morne / to speke be full fayne.
This is a great skorne / and a fals trane;
Now wols-hede and out-horne / on the be tane!
   Vile fature!
Oone worde myght thou speke ethe,
yit myght it do the som letht,
Et omni qui tacet
   hic consentire videtur.
Speke on oone word / right in the dwyllys name!
where was thi syre at bord / when he met with thi dame?
what, nawder bowted ne spurd / and a lord of name!
Speke on in a torde / the dwill gif the shame.

(136—48)

It occurs to Caiaphas that Jesus may be too frightened to speak
coherently. The exasperated priest will settle for a syllable:
"Great wordis has thou spokyn / then was thou not dom. / Be it
hole worde or brokyn / com, owt with som" (173—74). The men-

tion of a "brokyn" word in this context might conceivably evoke the fraction of the Host.

Recognizing that his colleague is becoming frantic, Annas attempts to calm him and presents an alternative plan for achieving the end they both desire: "It is best that we trete hym / with farenes. . . . And so myght we gett hym / som word for to say" (217–18). The priests may not strike Jesus so long as he remains silent. Annas turns to the captive and pursues a new, more reasonable line of questioning.

> Say, did thou oght this yll? / can thou oght excuse the?
> why standys thou so styll / when men thus accuse the?
> ffor to hyng on a hyll / hark how thay ruse the
>   To dam.
> Say, art thou godys son of heuen,
> As thou art wonte for to neuen?
>
> (245–50)

In response to this last question, Jesus speaks for the first and only time in the play.

> So thou says by thy steuen,
>   And right so I am;
> ffor after this shall thou se / when that [I] do com downe
> In brightnes on he / in clowdys from abone.
>
> (251–54)

Not until his interlocutors speak the truth do they merit a response. Only when Annas has—however unwittingly—applied his speech to the service of the Word does Jesus choose to serve him by speaking, as the Father has served the patriarchs and prophets who were the Word's vehicles. Jesus acknowledges that he is God's son. He will return to his Father's house, but he will also descend repeatedly thence to the altars of this earth.

From the priests' viewpoint, Jesus' speech is the confession they have sought. They decide to commit Jesus to the Tortores. With boisterous delight, the tormentors set about their work: "We shall preue on his crowne / the wordys he has saide" (363). Nobody "bot the fader that hym gate" (366) will be displeased by his suffering! Only Froward, the Tortores' servant, is less than enthusiastic about his work: "I haue had mekyll shame / hunger and thurst, / In youre seruyce" (382–83). As elsewhere in the cycle, particularly in the Wakefield Master plays, the theme of hunger and thirst signals disruption in the created hierarchy.

Further, like the hunger of Cain's Garcio, Noah's Uxor, and the shepherd Daw, Froward's physical hunger suggests the spiritual emptiness whose only remedy is the spiritual food of the Eucharist. The bloody sacrifice commemorated in that sacrament now begins as Jesus is beaten, taunted, and driven like a beast back to the priests and onward to Pilate.

Pilate's speech, opening the *Fflagellacio*, serves to reemphasize the judge's enmity to the Word. As before, he blasphemously advances his own word as absolute. More forcibly than his opening tirade in the *Conspiracio*, the speech emphasizes Pilate's "heretical" devotion to untruth: "I am full of sotelty, / ffalshed, gyll, and trechery" (10–11). As a judge, Pilate should uphold the truth, yet he delivers a rodomontade vaunting his techniques for finding "truth" wherever his material advantage lies.

> The right side to socoure, certys, I am full bayn,
>   If I may get therby a vantage or wynyng;
> Then to the fals parte I turn me agayn,
>   ffor I se more Vayll will to me be risyng.
>
> (16–19)

This might have been seen as a sly glance at such Lollard adjustable consciences as Cain manifests, or even at the Lollard penchant for serial recantations. Pilate continues by naming, as his servants and "dere darlyngys" (38), "fals endytars" (23), "men that vse bak-bytyngys, / and rasars of slaunderyngys" (36–37). It is against Jesus that Pilate plans to turn his "wordys of vanyte" (32), although—or because—Jesus is "trew both in dedys and in sawes" (43).

When Jesus is brought before Pilate, the prisoner breaks his silence, but only to remind Pilate that even he wields no power but what God has accorded him. Rupert of Deutz, in *De victoria verbi Dei*, comments on Jesus' abstinence from self-defense. The Word Incarnate could surely have argued eloquently before Pilate for his innocence,

> nisi quod ille auditem non habebat, et ipse per sapientem quemdam fuerat praelocutus: "Ne effundas sermonem, ubi non est auditus (Eccli. XXXII)." Nobis haec scienda reservavit [if it were not the case that he (Pilate) had no hearing, and that it had been foretold of him (Jesus) by a certain wise man, "Do not pour out your words where there is no hearing" (Eccles. 32). He reserved these things to be understood by us].[18]

The Word wastes no words arguing or pleading before the deaf and unworthy Pilate. Rather, his silent and sacrificial Presence speaks out to the audience, establishing communion with those who are worthy.

Jesus is given to the Tortores to be scourged. As they beat him, they taunt, "Where on seruys this prophecy / thou tell vs in this case, / And all thi warkys of greatt mastry / thou shewed in dyuers place?" (143–44). What the tormentors do not realize is that Jesus did prophesy the very event in which they participate, and the suffering he now endures is among the greatest of his "warkys." The Tortores speak of the miracles he has brought about, first mentioning a typological transubstantiation: "Syrs, at the ffeste of architreclyn / this prophete he was; / Ther turnyd he water into wyn / that day he had such grace" (152–53). As additional tales are told of his powers, Jesus stands central, silent and bleeding, and a powerful Eucharistic icon is created. Its impact is enhanced when Jesus is crowned with thorns and the Secundus Tortor speaks a parody of an elevation prayer: "Hayll kyng! where was thou borne / sich worship for to wyn?" (235). "Ther will no mete do me goode / To he be hanged on a roode" (239–40), continues the Tortor in a still more direct sacramental allusion. The Eucharist itself is the "mete" that might do him good; further, popular belief attributed to attendance at Mass the virtue of making all food more nourishing.[19]

Preparations for the Crucifixion begin, while John and the three Marys share the woeful "tythyngys" (278) and approach the cross-bearing Jesus. Before these worthy listeners, Jesus speaks freely, consoling his mother by reminding her of his Resurrection to come, yet encouraging the women's lamentation for the terrible death he is to die. They are interrupted by the Tortores, who call Jesus' prophecy "vayn carpyng" (346) and wish that the women's "wordys" (350) might be silenced. With Simon's reluctant help, the cross is carried onward to Calvary.

The *Processus crucis* opens with yet another tirade from Pilate, who cries "peasse" repeatedly (1, 8, 9, 13) as a prelude to the imminent terrible scene of violence. The Tortores discuss Jesus' "lies," the "prowde wordys" (45) by which he has merited the death they are preparing for him. The Primus Tortor boasts that Jesus "shall with all his mawmentry / No longere vs be tell" (78–79): Jesus' "idolatry" will not serve him now. Along with the sharp irony of these lines comes an encoded counter-Lollard message, for "mawmentry" was a characteristic term among

Lollards, one they often used to describe the actions of orthodox clerics.[20] As the Tortores taunt and torment him, Jesus remains a silent and powerful image of the redemptive sacrifice.

Only when Jesus has been nailed to the cross and the cross stands upright does he break silence.

> I pray you pepyll that passe me by,
> That lede youre lyfe so lykandly,
> heyfe vp your hartys on hight!
> Behold if euer ye sagh body
> Buffet & bett thus blody,
> Or yet thus dulfully dight;
> In warld was neuer no wight
> That suffred half so sare.
> My mayn, my mode, my myght,
> Is noght bot sorow to sight,
> And comforth none, bot car.

(233–43)

Inviting attention to his sacrificial appearance, Jesus invokes the identity of the Crucifixion with the sacrifice of the Mass. The moment of spiritual communion by visual contact with the consecrated Host is a re-creation of this dramatized "historical moment" when the crucified Jesus spoke. The Word present in the sacrament is a silent one, yet the ritual communicates the same message as does Jesus' speech from the cross.

The Crucifixion's sacramental reference is further stressed in Mary's conversation with John at the foot of the cross. Jesus is referred to as a "foode."

> [Maria.] My foode that I haue fed,
> In lyf longyng the led,
> fful stratly art thou sted
> Emanges thi foo-men fell.

(313–16)

> [Iohannes.] he was thi fode, thi faryst foine,
> Thi luf, thi lake, thi lufsom son.

(343–44)

> [Maria.] My frely foode now farys me fro / what shall worth on me?

(412)

Mary also refers to Jesus as her "lam" (391); and, in a context that may recall the tradition of elevation visions of bleeding flesh, she dwells upon his body's appearance.

> To deth my dere is dryffen,
> his robe is all to-ryffen,
> That of me was hym gyffen,
> And shapen with my sydys.

(386–89)

Incrementally, the spectators' attention is drawn to the sacramental extension of the event they are witnessing.

Jesus speaks his last words before death, commending his soul to his Father, and the play draws to its close. The blind Longeus, his sight miraculously restored, recapitulates the action's meaning: "I se thou hyngys here on hy, / And dyse to fulfyll the prophecy" (605–6). With the spotlight, however briefly, on Longeus, the spectators may be invited to recollect the traditional belief that the sight of the elevated Host preserves them from blindness.[21]

The Passion is "broght tyll ende" (590), but the sequence continues with the *Processus talentorum*, an anticlimactic play—it would seem—whose inclusion requires clarification. Arnold Williams suggests that the play's purpose is

> to add the last and finishing touches to the character of Pilate. If that is its purpose, no one can doubt its success, for the Procurator of Judea here sketched is a crafty, unscrupulous fellow, not above using his power to browbeat a common soldier out of his winnings in a game of chance.[22]

Like the *Magnus Herodes*, the play appears to celebrate evil's triumph, the triumph of the anti-Word: Jesus is dead, and Pilate endures, more bombastic than ever. In mixed Latin and English, he opens the play with the familiar demand for silence and assertions of his great attributes and powers. In their commentary on the play's text, A. C. Cawley and Martin Stevens gloss the opening lines thus: "Notice, you who stand [by] that I am of wondrous valour; / know this, I will slay you unless you keep quiet. / Learn, all of you, that I am a man of god-like nature / and majesty; do not harm me by speaking, / thus I command. / Be neither talkative / nor garrulous, / demand peace / while I speak."[23] In his efforts to silence his listeners, he manifests the enmity to the Word that we have seen in earlier ranting rulers.

"Qui bene wlt fari [glossed by Cawley and Stevens as "he who wishes to speak well"][24] / shuld call me fownder of all lay" (22): Pilate permits only such speech as would declare him godlike. Yet this Pilate also appears to recognize the Word's potential power over him ("do not harm me by speaking"). After all, language is all Pilate has. As Theresa Coletti asserts, "For Pilate, language is power, and the proper response to authority is silence. . . . This emphasis on language and silence suggests the implicit contrast between those individual human utterances that Pilate can control and God's utterance, Christ, the incarnate Word that cannot be silenced and whose seamless coat cannot be divided."[25] Pilate's authority, like that of foregoing Towneley tyrants, is thoroughly undercut by the play's contrastive design.

The play's action concerns Christ's "cote"—which cannot, indeed, be divided—and the efforts of Pilate and each of the three Tortores to win it for himself. What is this "cote," one must wonder, and what is the point of the men's eagerness to acquire it? Like the "robe" Mary speaks of in the *Processus crucis* (387), this is not the body's garment, but the body itself, intact and indestructible, despite all the violence of the Passion.[26] Woolf suggests that, if the robe is understood to be Christ's body, the play depicts "evildoers or in particular gamesters who rend Christ's body, the Church, or crucify him anew."[27] This dramatic action may also function to condemn inroads—such as those perpetrated by the Lollards—upon the Church's integrity, while it simultaneously reinforces belief in the beleaguered sacrament. Coletti indeed notes that "biblical commentators [on the robe] frequently emphasized the indivisible unity of *corpus Christi* by referring to those heretics who profane both Scripture and the sacraments yet cannot disturb the bond of charity that Christ's body in its oneness represents."[28]

The Primus Tortor, explaining his desire to possess the "cote," describes its value thus:

> ffor whosoeuer may get thise close,
> he ther neuer rek where he gose,
> ffor he semys nothyng to lose,
> If so be he theym were.

(105–8)

The Secundus Tortor is equally enthusiastic.

> ffor if I myght this cote gett,
> Then wold I both skyp and lepe,

And therto fast both drynke and ete,
In fayth, as I were mad.

(141–44)

The robe would be "right prophetabyll" (168) to the Tortores, they agree, resolving to keep it from Pilate. Its apparently magical attributes are similar to the "virtues" attributed by popular belief to the Eucharist. The Secundus Tortor's allusion to drinking and eating further supports the notion that the "cote" represents Christ's body in its sacramental manifestation. So does Secundus Tortor's very name, "Spyll-payn" (124), which Cawley and Stevens gloss as "waste-bread."[29] He and his fellows truly have wasted Christ, the Bread of Life. The pun functions doubly: the *Oxford English Dictionary* shows that *waste* could mean, then as now, both "destroy" and "squander." While they believe they have destroyed Christ, they have, in fact, squandered the opportunity for communion with him, a prodigality of which they will repent at play's end. The pattern of the preceding plays is sustained as this sacramental body, silent yet powerful, holds the center of an otherwise chaotic stage. Pilate's apparent triumph—a triumph of arbitrary human law and language—is sharply undercut by its presence, a Presence the audience knows to be eternally recurrent and eternally efficacious.

As the play continues, the four men dice for the robe. The Tercius Tortor wins, but Pilate bullies him into giving it up. With nothing further to win or lose, the Primus Tortor launches into a homily against gambling. He forswears the dice by which he was "neuer so happy / by mayn nor by mode, / To win with sich sotelty / to my lyfys fode" (370–71). The identity of the "cote" with the sacramental body remains focal. The Tortores have been perfectly correct in their recognition of the value and desirability of the robe. Where they have erred is in imagining that they might depend on Fortune (and Pilate) rather than on God for material and spiritual benefits they lacked. The Primus Tortor has come to realize that one cannot gain one's "lyfys fode"—be it material daily bread or the Eucharistic wafer—by gambling. Determining to "serue god herafter, / ffor heuens blys" (398–99), the Tortores have found the true path to their sustenance.

The final play before the climactic *Resurreccio* is the *Extraccio animarum*, the Harrowing of Hell. The debate begun in the Creation play comes at last to an end as Satan faces Jesus and is unequivocally defeated. The Word triumphs: in the delivery of the patriarchs and prophets from hell, the spectators find a potent visual image of his redemptive work. Jesus' opening speech summarizes the salvific plan. Humanity was won by the devil "thrugh fraude of earthly fode" (14), but the spiritual, sacramental food of the blood Jesus has shed will redeem them. Sending a light before him, he awakens the patriarchs and prophets to his coming, and they recall the significant events they have enacted and the prophecies that are now to be fulfilled. To them and to the distraught devils comes the sound of the omnipotent Word—spoken, like the liturgy, in Latin: "Attollite portas, principes, vestras & eleuamini porte eternales, & introibit rex glorie" (115).

With his Word, Christ bursts open the gates of hell. As Woolf points out, however, "Christ's verbal defeat of the devil is a far more impressive symbol of the victory of the redemption than his token destruction of the gates of hell."[30] Answering Satan's every argument, Jesus demonstrates that "ilke true prophete tayll / shalbe fulfillid in me" (287–88). The just souls who have been confined in hell "shall pas vnto the place of peasse" (310)—true peace, not a tyrant's repression—and their redemption prefigures that of all who follow his law and his "sacramentys" (336). Satan attempts to defy him, but the Word's triumph is simply and powerfully dramatized.

> *Ihesus.* Devill, I commaunde the to go downe
>   into thi sete where thou shall syt.
> *Sathan.* Alas, for doyll and care!
>   I synk into hell pyt!

> (357–60)

Christ leads his "childer" (363) from hell. The history of the life and death of the Word Incarnate is completed, and the triumph of his return from death foretold. With the *Resurreccio domini*, the cycle will move into a phase of direct concentration on the Word's continuance beyond Jesus' earthly life, the Word as sacrament.

7
Sacramental Fulfillment of the Word

In the development of its orthodox theme, the fulfillment of God's Word, the Towneley cycle gradually brings the Eucharist into ever greater prominence and clearer focus. The audience's liturgical experience is a constant point of reference: at any moment in the unfolding cycle, a contemporary devotional analogue to the dramatized events is available. Not until the *Resurreccio domini* and its successors, however, does the Eucharist become the central and direct focus of the cycle's embodiment of Christian theology. In this final group of plays, the Word is depicted in its sacramental fulfillment. The Eucharist is instituted in a purposively extrabiblical presentation, and specific tenets of the sacrament's theology are given dramatic expression. These plays, like their predecessors in the Passion sequence, have primarily positive counter-Lollard content, powerfully suggesting the joys of orthodoxy rather than concentrating on the woes of heresy. Sensitized audience members, attracted to or frightened by what they knew of Lollardy, would see some direct suggestions of heretical behavior in these plays. But what these spectators would find dominant and most forceful is the plays' continuing enactment of the sacrament, of its power to appease the hungers of this world and its salvific instrumentality.

The treatment of the sacrament's institution demands careful consideration. As has frequently been pointed out, the Corpus Christi cycles' depiction of the historical institution at the Last Supper is not as prominent as might be expected. Alan H. Nelson states the problem:

> We may wish to conceive of the cycle plays as an elaboration of the Passion; but is it really possible to understand them as essentially an elaboration of the Eucharist? Hardison notes that the Last Supper is not even included in Kolve's protocycle of plays common to the cycles. It is true that the Last Supper does occur in all the extant cycles: Kolve subsumes it under the category of the Passion. But the

Institution of the Eucharist is quite absent from the Wakefield and possibly from the York cycle. Nor does it rise to great prominence in the Chester cycle. The N-Town cycle, which makes most of the Eucharist, is announced for "sunday next," and thus was not, and may never have been, intended for the Corpus Christi occasion.[1]

In the context of the cycle's potential as a counter-Lollard force, how are we to explain such a startling apparent de-emphasis of the embattled sacrament? Does the Towneley cycle's failure to depict the Eucharist's institution at the Last Supper detract from the drama's antiheretical force or, indeed, undercut the argument that the drama embodied such force? The Towneley cycle does not, it is true, depict the historical moment of the institution, but the omission may actually be seen to serve the cycle's overall effect of bolstering sacramental orthodoxy. The institution is dramatized, but outside its historical moment in a context in which both doctrinal clarity and dramatic impact are assured.

Christ's institution of the Eucharist at the Last Supper is indubitably a significant historical and theological event. Its theological importance resides in certain aspects of the event that contribute to primary tenets of Eucharistic theology. Christ himself instituted the sacrament, prescribing, as it were, its liturgical form, although the Lollards would argue otherwise.[2] The historical institution took the form of a communal meal, Christ's sharing of himself with his Apostles, the earliest Church. These aspects of the institution underlie the theological clarification of transubstantiation, the Real Presence, and the meaning of Eucharistic communion. That the institution took place at the last earthly supper Christ was to share with his followers bears a weighty meaning. This finality evokes the sacrament's eschatological meaning: the Eucharist, for communicants in a state of grace, is a foretaste of the celestial banquet; it is preeminently the sacrament of salvation. Further, in the Pauline formulation, it is the seal of damnation for those receiving it unworthily.

These ideas—that of the Real Presence and that of communion, with its immediate and eschatological effects—are central aspects of Eucharistic theology. As such, they must be emphasized in a cycle celebrating Corpus Christi and reinforcing orthodox devotion. They need not receive this emphasis, however, in the context of the historical Last Supper's depiction. In fact, a dramatist might consciously have sought an alternative approach, for the third central meaning of the Eucharist—the sacrificial meaning—cannot easily be depicted with full clarity in the context of this event.

It is doctrinally true, albeit paradoxical, that the Passion, which had not yet happened, was commemorated in the Eucharist's first celebration.[3] The mortal audience exists in linear time, however, and there is surely potential confusion for that audience in the notion of present commemoration of a future event. This potential confusion may be illustrated by an extract from the banns of the Chester cycle.

> And howe Criste, our sauioure at his laste supper
> Gaue his bodye and bloode for redemtion of us all
> yow Bakers see yat with the same wordes you vtter
> As Criste himselfe spake them to be a memorall /
> Of yat deathe & passion within playe after ensue shall.[4]

The twisted syntax of this passage is not mere poetic left-footedness, although it is certainly that. More importantly, it speaks eloquently to the difficulty of communicating the Eucharist's full meaning in the context of its institution. To emphasize the historical institution is, potentially, to run the risk of suggesting that the sacrament commemorates *only* the Last Supper and not the Passion itself.

Variation in the scriptural accounts of the Last Supper illuminates the Towneley cycle's treatment of the event. The descriptions of the paschal meal in the three synoptic Gospels and in 1 Corinthians all depict Christ's institution of the Eucharist.[5] In the three Gospels, the sacrificial nature of the observance is stressed through prophetic allusions. That is, it is evident to the Christian reader of the Gospels; it may be argued that it was not so to the participating Apostles.[6] Paul's retelling of the event refers to the sacrament as commemoration of the death, which is also a past event from the writer's viewpoint. John's Gospel, despite the considerable length of its account of the Last Supper, does not depict the institution. The Gospel does, however, contain an earlier discourse (John 6:26–59) expressing the promise of the sacrament and its doctrinal meanings, including the sacrificial significance.

In this Gospel's unique presentation of the Last Supper, the Towneley dramatist may have found both suggestion and warrant for his own treatment.[7] Thus, the dramatist was operating within a conventional context in choosing his approach. Significantly, the Gospel reading for the Mass of Maundy Thursday was drawn from John (13:1–15). Further, the tradition of pictorial art throughout the Middle Ages portrayed the Last Supper far more frequently as a tableau of betrayal than as the moment of the sacrament's institution.[8] The issue, then, is not the play's unconventionality, but the effect of the choice of one convention over another.

The action's probable derivation from John rather than the synoptic Gospels precludes confusion in the spectators' minds as to what the sacrament commemorates. The Last Supper in the Towneley cycle occurs in the *Conspiracio*, 314–487, framed on the one side by Judas's selling of his master to Caiaphas and by the agony on "olyuete" on the other. The rising action of the play concerns the betrayal and the immediate anticipation of the Passion. Although it would certainly have been possible to include the institution in a play depicting these events—the N-Town Passion, with its multiple acting loci, manages this splendidly—the Towneley cycle takes a different course. The cycle lets the Passion speak for itself, only later presenting the Eucharist that must be understood in its light. Thus potential doctrinal confusion is avoided, a confusion likely to have preexisted in the minds of those spectators who had been touched by Lollard denial of the Real Presence. Those Lollards who argued that there was no transubstantiation and no Real Presence asserted therefore that the sacrament could not be a true sacrifice.[9] The Towneley approach also enhances the audience's sense of knowledgeable participation in events unfolding for the first time. Like the Apostles at the Last Supper, the audience cannot fully understand the meaning of the Eucharist until the prophecies of death and resurrection have been fulfilled. The cycle withholds the Eucharist for a moment at which its full meaning can be apprehended without the intervention of prophecy. That moment is the Resurrection.

*   *   *

The dramatic center of the Towneley *Resurreccio domini* is the Resurrection itself and Christ's monologue, in which the Word is sacramentally fulfilled. The prelude to this moment briefly recapitulates previously established themes of the Word. Contrasting "janglyng" deceit with powerfully simple "trowth," the prelude prepares the audience for the Word's Resurrection and his ahistorical institution of the sacrament by which the Word is perpetuated through all time.

Pilate opens the play with the now-familiar rant. "Peasse" (1), he cries; "Spare youre spech . . . / And sesse youre cry" (7–8). Demanding attention to his own speech, he issues threats to any who attend to the words of the slain prophet: "If ther be any that blow such bost, / with tormentys keyn bese he indost / ffor euermore" (32–34). Caiaphas reassures Pilate that there will be no trouble from Jesus' followers, for Centurio has been left at Calvary to arrest troublemakers. Centurio, however, casts an ironic light back over Caiaphas's speech with his own opening words. The patriarchal phrase, "A, blyssyd lord adonay" (45), alerts the audience immediately to the fact that Centurio is not of the party of the heretical judge and priests.

Although the debate in hell between Christ and Satan represents a final triumph of the Word, the debate still rages on earth: the individual is free to follow or ignore the redemptive Word. The contrast between the speeches of Pilate and Centurio bears witness to this continuing tension between good and evil, a tension that was certainly felt in the audience's contemporary world. As before, the good is defined as truth, that is, orthodoxy, and Centurio is its spokesman.

> Oure prynces, for sothe, dyd nothyng right,
> And so I saide to theym on hight,
> > As it is trew,
> That he was most of myght,
> The son of god, ihesu.
>
> (58–62)

Likewise, as before, evil is depicted as falsehood, denial of truth, and the equation with heresy remains implicit, although the contemporary Lollard is not directly evoked. Pilate asks to hear Centurio's "tythyngys" (81). When he does, however, the judge's automatic response is, "Centurio, sese of sich saw" (92). Centurio, a new protopriest for the cycle, persists in his desire to "mayntene trowth" (98) and repeats his assertion of Christ's divinity. The debate continues; the evil characters employ their characteristic technique of referring to the Word as "lesyngys" (141) and issuing to its vehicle a command for silence, "Hold styll thy clattur" (145). Perceiving that he cannot change their minds, Centurio departs, voicing the charitable wish, "God lene you grace to knaw / the sothe all way" (147).

The moment is ripe for a triumphant dramatic reversal, yet the playwright does not, indeed cannot effect a simple shift to a mood of glorious triumph. Pamela Sheingorn provides compelling analysis of the artistic and theological traditions that the Resurrection playwrights inherited. In the dramatic icons they created, "the dramatists were referring to two visual images, each the product of a distinct theological tradition. One, that of Christ rising triumphantly from his tomb, is based on the 'abuse of power' or 'classic' theory of the Atonement. The other, that of the *Imago pietatis*, or Man of Sorrows, a *Christus patiens* figure, took impetus from a newer theory of the Atonement that emphasized Christ's humanity."[10] The Towneley play participates in both of these traditions by stressing the Image of Pity in Christ's long monologue, allowing the audience to concentrate on his humanity and sacrifice, while simultaneously expressing the theme of triumph through an elevation—historically the first—of the sacrament. The play invites the spectators to relieve through sacramental communion the agonized tension of having witnessed the Passion.

In the Resurrection scene, then, as in so many previous episodes, the action invokes the audience's liturgical experience to dramatic and markedly counter-Lollard didactic effect. While depicting a historical moment, the scene also powerfully recalls the spectators' personal experience of the Eucharist, particularly their participation in the rites of Easter day. On that day, medieval Christians experienced their closest and most absorbing involvement with the sacrament: Easter Mass was the occasion for most laypersons' single annual sacramental communion. Further, the elaborate and impressive preliminary rite of that Mass involved the "resurrection" of the Host, Christ's body, from its "sepulcher" and the singing of the anthem, "Christus resurgens."[11] Although a chorus of angels was believed to be present at every consecration,[12] the angels in this scene and their song, "Christus resurgens," specifically evoke the Easter Mass. The dramatization of Jesus' rising from the tomb—which is also his elevation from the altar—works to vivify the audience's understanding of that Mass, demonstrating the identity of the resurrected body they have seen in church, the Host, with the body resurrected once for all time on the first Easter morning.

Having witnessed the Passion and Resurrection, the spectators are now prepared to receive the sacrament in full understanding. It is at this ideal psychological moment that the Eucharist is instituted in the Towneley cycle. As Sheingorn points out, Christ's speaking role in this play (unlike the Passion sequence) creates a moment "outside historical time."[13] Thus it is not necessary that the imagery of the suffering Christ be abandoned for the scene to convey triumph—the central Christian triumph of life over death. What is presented as triumphant here is not the historical Jesus rising from the tomb—that figure remains largely one of pathos—but the extrahistorical continuation of him in the glorious Eucharist. The Word, Christ's flesh, made present as if in the sacrament, is endowed in the scene with a speaking voice addressed to the audience.

> . . . I am veray prynce of peasse,
> And synnes seyr I may releasse,
> And whoso will of synnes seasse
>   And mercy cry,
> I graunt theym here a measse
>   In brede, my awne body.
>
> That ilk veray brede of lyfe
> Becommys my flesche in wordys fyfe;
> who so it resaues in syn or stryfe
>   Bese ded for euer;
> And whoso it takys in rightwys lyfe
>   Dy shall he neuer.
>
>   (322–33)

Walter E. Meyers points out that while one hundred lines of Jesus' monologue in this play "are taken word-for-word from a religious lyric poem 'The Dollorus complant of oure lorde Apoune the croce Crucifyit,'" the lines here cited are probably original with the dramatist.[14] The interpolation's conventional statement of sacramental doctrine[15] would have been, as discussed at the beginning of this chapter, potentially confusing in the context of the Last Supper and the rising tension of the Passion sequence, where it could not have achieved a climactic impact. Here in the *Resurreccio* it is both doctrinally clear and dramatically powerful. The emphasis on the "wordys fyfe" of consecration especially serves to evoke the momentum of the cycle's concern with the Word and to exhort devoted attention to orthodox ritual.

The sacrificial nature of the sacrament is realized far more effectively in this context than it could have been in that of the Last Supper. Here, when Jesus grants the Mass of his "awne body," the spectators can see that he is speaking of the sacrificed body. While we may be fairly certain that the actor playing this role, in the age of late medieval affective piety, was realistically made up with blood and wounds, the text alone makes the body—the Image of Pity—focal in this scene.[16]

> Behold my body, in ilka place
>   how it was dight;

> All to-rent and all to-shentt,
>   Man, for thy plight.
>
> (246–49)

> Behald my shankes and my knees,
> Myn armes and my thees;
> Behold me well, looke what thou sees,
>   Bot sorow and pyne. . . .
>
> (262–65)

> Behold my body how Iues it dang
> with knottys of whyppys and scorges strang;
> As stremes of well the bloode out sprang
>   On euery syde.
>
> . . . .
> In body, heed, feete, and hand,
> ffour hundreth woundys and fyve thowsand
>   here may thou se;
> And therto neyn were delt full euen
>   ffor luf of the.
>
> (274–77, 281–85)

This is the body of which the faithful partake in the Mass: the body sacrificed for them. Thus, the Towneley cycle does depict Jesus instituting the Eucharist—not at the Last Supper in the presence of Apostles who understand it only through the shadows of prophecy—but after the Resurrection and as a direct presentation to the audience, who are now in a position fully to understand the gift's significance and appreciate the experience granted them. Theresa Coletti, in her analysis of the N-Town Passion, makes a point that is equally relevant to the Towneley *Resurreccio*: "If the stories of the living Host give testimony to the desire to see evidence of Christ's fleshly nature in the Eucharist," the play "fulfills that desire, offering opportunities for contemplation of the sacrament as well as visible reassurance of Christ's presence in it."[17]

The resurrected Word continues to speak in explanation of the instituted sacrament. To understand the Eucharist's sacrificial meaning is to understand not only that the sacrifice has been offered but also that it is motivated by divine love. Divine love, visually realized in Jesus' sacrificial appearance and expressed in his speech, cries out for a return of love.

> Into this dongeon depe I soght
> And all for luf of the.
>
> (230–31)

> Thou must me luf that thus gaf than
>   My lyfe for thyne.
>
> (242–43)

> here may thou se that I luf the,
>   Man, faythfully.
>
> (290–91)

> Sen I for luf, man, boght the dere,
> As thou thi self the sothe sees here,
> I pray the hartely, with good chere,
>   luf me agane.
>
> (292–95)

> That I great luf ay to the had,
>   well may thou knaw!
> Som luf agane I wold full fayn
>   Thou wold me shaw.
>
> (312–15)

Humanity is to "lyf in charyte / Both nyght and day" (318–19) to reciprocate the Redeemer's love. Although no direct connection is drawn between this "charyte" and the Eucharistic observance, the monologue's juxtaposition of these ideas is likely to have influenced the spectator toward this connection. To partake of the Eucharist is to obey Jesus' precept and thereby to return his love. This connection is to be drawn explicitly in the later *Thomas Indie*. The Eucharist is instituted in the *Resurreccio* such that it may be fully understood as a sacrifice, impelled by love and transmitting mercy, that asks a return of love. The sacrament is thus portrayed, in a powerfully counter-Lollard formulation, as the sine qua non of Christian life.

In the institution of the Eucharist by the bleeding, resurrected Christ, doctrine is dramatically embodied: the sacrificial nature of the sacrament is acutely realized, and the love informing the sacrifice is clearly expressed. But this is only the cycle's first step toward the comprehensive embodiment of Eucharistic doctrine. In the *Resurreccio*, the doctrines of transubstantiation and the Real Presence, as well as the immediate and eschatological meanings of the sacrament for the communicant, are stated; but their dramatic embodiment is reserved for a more effective moment in the unfolding drama. The three plays that follow the *Resurreccio*—the *Peregrini*, the *Thomas Indie*, and the *Ascencio*—vivify the Real Presence as dramatically as does the earlier play the redemptive sacrifice. The audience is made to understand that direct communion with the sacrificed and resurrected Christ, which they have experienced as spectators of the *Resurreccio*, is theirs at every Mass by virtue of the Real Presence and the effects of recurrent communion, spiritual or sacramental.

It is in the *Peregrini* that the Mass granted in the *Resurreccio* is first celebrated. The play opens with a long lamentation alternating between Cleophas and Luke, the burden of which is their grief for their tortured and murdered Lord. What is missing from this lamentation—the flaw in the pilgrims' orthodoxy—is certainty of the Resurrection and of the enduring presence of Christ among his followers. It would appear that the Passion has "spoken for itself" only too well for its onstage audience. The pilgrims are suffering from a spiritual malady; they are in need of the "leche" lamented by Luke at line 17. When Jesus enters at line 98, his speeches serve as a corrective to the pilgrims' blind grief. He so consoles them that they implore him in the name of "charite" (241) to remain with them as they stop for the night.

The meal then shared among the three turns out to be a Mass, as the stage directions—and, no doubt, the staging itself—make clear.

> *Tunc recumbent & sedebit ihesus in medio eorum, tunc benedicet ihesus panem & franget in tribus partibus, & postea euanebit ab oculis eorum. . . .* [Then they go to the table, and Jesus sits between them; then Jesus blesses the bread and breaks it in three parts and afterward vanishes from their sight. . . .] (following 190)

While the play is largely faithful to the Gospel account of this event (Luke 24:13–32), the sacramental reference of the bread's being broken *in three parts* is the playwright's addition, although not his invention. The *Glossa ordinaria* interprets this event at the pilgrims' supper as communion, referring to the bread Jesus breaks as "sacramentum panis."[18] The connection is also suggested in art: medieval pictorial depictions of the supper at Emmaus are often designed to recall the sacramental institution at the Last Supper.[19] Finally, the liturgy itself implies the episode's sacramental significance. The sequence for the Mass of Monday after Easter concludes with a paean to the "living bread" of the Eucharist; it is followed immediately by the Gospel account of the events at Emmaus.[20] Speaking of the tripartite breaking of the bread, Meyers suggests:

> This borrowing from the liturgy is inserted into the play to continue the emphasis on the Mass begun in the *Resurrection* play. The Eu-

charistic meal is the evidence of Christ's continued presence; it is how the audience, as well as Cleophas and Luke, "recognizes" Him.[21]

The sacramental detail is enhanced by the stage directions' suggestion that Jesus vanishes immediately after the breaking of the bread, although he apparently remains just long enough to give it to the pilgrims and be recognized, as in Luke 24:30-31. Saint Thomas Aquinas asserts that the reality of the Real Presence is not and cannot be a visible reality. Thomas draws an analogy, however, between Christ's appearance to the pilgrims at Emmaus and the appearance to believers of a child or flesh in the place of the Host. In both cases, God has formed an image in the beholder's eye to communicate the presence of an invisible truth.[22]

What the dramatic action suggests here is that the bread, blessed and broken by Jesus, has become the sacramental species, the visible accidents of which clothe the invisible substance of the Corpus Christi. This juxtaposition of the visible presence of Christ with his disappearance—as it were, into the sacramental species—effectively and dramatically expresses the doctrines of transubstantiation and the Real Presence. The episode's sacramental significance is reinforced in the play's concluding section by the pilgrims' repeated references to the breaking of the bread. In the Gospel, the pilgrims tell the other Apostles how Jesus "was known to them in the breaking of the bread" (Luke 24:35). The playwright stresses this detail.

> I had no knawlege it was he,
> Bot for he brake this brede in thre. . . .
>
> (328–29)

> ffro he toke breede full well I wyst,
> And brake it here with his awne fyste,
> And laide it vs at his awne lyst,
>   As we it hent;
> I knew hym then, and sone it kyst
>   with good intente.
>
> (340–45)

Not only does the episode emphasize the pilgrims' recognition of Jesus by his sacramental action; it also suggests, in the final lines quoted above, that Cleophas has completed the celebration of the sacrament by "kissing" the bread "with good intente." While this phrasing may suggest communion directly, it may also bring to the spectator's mind the ceremonial kissing of the *os-culatorium* or *pax-brede*, which occurred during the Mass just before communion. This ritual, deriving from the Kiss of Peace shared among worshipers preparing themselves for communion in the primitive church, was increasingly invested with the full significance of communion in the later Middle Ages, when the sacramental communion of the laity became infrequent.[23] The pilgrims become active first as participants in a communion ritual, and then, cured of their paralyzing grief, as disseminators of the Word: having taken in the Word, they can now transmit it to others. As the play ends, Luke and Cleophas, spiritually healed and strengthened by the Eucharistic celebration, are hurrying to Jerusalem to share their experience with the other Apostles. The spectator is left with enhanced reverence for the contemporary priest who will break the bread for them and for the ritual that effects the interpenetration of the scriptural world and their own.

In the next play, *Thomas Indie*, the need for faith in the unseen is the central thematic concern. The scriptural story of Doubting Thomas exhorts faith in the Resurrection, but the Towneley play is loaded with Eucharistic reference. In the play's first half, in which Jesus appears three times to the assembled Apostles, a proto-Mass is again celebrated, and its effects on the communicating Apostles are evidenced in their later interaction with Thomas. The depiction of Thomas's incredulity and its resolution is not a simple—or simpleminded—repetition of what has already been demonstrated in the cases of the other Apostles. The episode allows for a more extensive depiction than that in the *Peregrini* of activity spurred by Eucharistic nourishment. Further, Thomas's experience—that of an individual straying from orthodoxy—holds valuable lessons for individual spectators. His characterization—like that of Cain much earlier in the cycle—is structured to move the audience from sympathetic identification with a man of heretical leanings toward an alienation partly determined by their sense of their own superior faith. Having been able to believe without seeing, they are reinforced in their awareness that their communion experience supersedes even the visual and tactile contact with Jesus that Thomas demands.

The play opens with Mary Magdalen's annunciation to Peter and Paul of the joyful news of the Resurrection. Paul's appearance is extrabiblical, and his antifeminist tirade (29–52) in response to Mary's declaration may seem, to a modern reader, gratuitous; still, the speech contributes to the play's exploration of weak or flawed faith. The play provides no smooth transition into Peter's lamentation for Jesus (65–79), and this suggests that two discrete plays have been spliced at this point.[24] The splicer was not inept, however, for, had we a pause, a scene change, between these sections, the transition would be plausible and effective. Peter, having once absorbed Mary's news, would naturally turn to reflection over his shameful denial of his master, the master he must soon face. Entering into Peter's state of mind, the audience is subtly prepared for Jesus' entrance. Vicariously, the scene becomes, for the spectator, a rehearsal for Judgment.

Following Peter's lamentation, Paul speaks his own, which recalls those of Luke and Cleophas in the preceding play.

> Now ihesu, for thi lyfe swete / who hath mastryd the?
> That in the breede that we eytt / thi self gyffen wold be;
> And sythen thrugh handys and feytt / be nalyd on a tre;
> Grauntt vs grace that we may yit / thi light in manhede se.
>
> (80–83)

Yet this lament, with its Eucharistic reference, represents a significant advance over those of the pilgrims. Although Paul is not ready to relinquish the sight of Jesus "in manhede," he is aware of the Eucharistic gift through which Jesus' continuing, if invisible, Presence is assured. It is surely no coincidence that Jesus' first appearance in the play follows directly upon these lines: it is as if Paul's reference to the sacrament has invoked him.

At his first appearance, Jesus sings "*pax vobis*" to the Apostles, then disappears. The Apostles, believing they have had a vision, pray to see Christ in the flesh. He appears again, and again his followers pray to see him bodily, believing that they have not yet done so. Eleanor Prosser argues that "this double appearance, used also at York, is a piece of mere stage trickery for its own sake. The repetition seems to have neither doctrinal nor dramatic purpose."[25] On the contrary, the repetition serves both doctrinal and dramatic ends. It evokes the spectators' liturgical experience, vivifying for them the Mass of the Tuesday after Easter. Therein, Christ's appearance to the disciples with his gift of "peace" is twice recalled.[26] The spectators, as so often before, are given the opportunity to equate scriptural characters' historical interaction with Jesus and their own experience of the Mass.

Here at last is the true "peasse," antithetical to the "peasse" of repression and error cried by Pilate and other evildoers. The repetition also functions thematically: the necessity for Jesus' reappearance stresses the weakness of the Apostles' faith at this

historical moment. Jesus' second disappearance is followed by a
speech from one of the Apostles that includes these lines:

> Mightfull god shelde vs fro shame / In thi moder name marie;
> Thise wykid Iues will vs blame / Thou grauntt vs for to se
> The self body and the same / the which that died on tre.
>
> (93–95)

If the body is not made visible, the "wykid Iues" will, presumably, continue to deny the Resurrection and persecute the
Apostles. "Wykid" may even fleetingly suggest "Wycliffite": to
be sure, the "Iues" might be converted by a sight of the resurrected body just as Lollards were converted by elevation visions.

The Apostle is praying for exactly that faith-strengthening experience which was vouchsafed to the audience in the *Resurreccio:* contact with the Corpus Christi, the body of sacrifice, a
necessary first step toward personally redemptive participation
in the sacrifice. The word "grauntt" here, as well as in Paul's
earlier speech, may specifically recall Jesus' "I grauntt theym
here a measse" in the Resurrection play (326). The verbal echo
strengthens the connection between the experience the Apostles
desire and the spectators' communion experience. Although
there can be little doubt that the audience appreciated the "stage
trickery" involved in Jesus' appearances, doctrinal concerns are
preeminent in the episode.

Upon Jesus' third appearance, the Apostles' desire is fulfilled:
the resurrected Christ grants his followers both visual and physical contact with the body of sacrifice. In his speech, as earlier in
the *Resurreccio,* Jesus conveys the caritas implicit in this contact. Communion with the body of sacrifice draws the Christian
inside the divine love that enjoined both Passion and Resurrection.

> luf makys me, as ye may se / strenkyllid with blood so red;
> luf gars me haue hart so fre / it opyns euery sted;
> luf so fre so dampnyd me / it drofe me to the ded;
> luf rasid me thrug his pauste / it is swetter than med.
>
> (108–11)

The communicant becomes not only the passive recipient of
caritas but its active transmitter to others.[27] The meal following
this speech, based on a brief statement in Luke 24:41–43, is
amplified and shaped to demonstrate the connection between
communion and active charity.

Unlike the meal in the *Peregrini*, this repast is not characterized by properties or gestures as a Mass. Jesus blesses the food,
fish and honey, in the names of the Trinity. No overt suggestion is
made that he is consecrating sacramental species. However, Jesus
then invites the Apostles to share the meal with him, and, significantly, this invitation is the playwright's extrabiblical addition.

> My dere freyndys lay hand till / eyttys for charite;
> I ette at my fader will / at my will ette now ye.
> That I ette is to fulfill / that writen is of me
> In moyses law, for it is skyll / ffulfillyd that it be.
>
> Myn ye noght that I you told / in certan tyme and sted,
> When I gaf myself to wold / to you in fourme of bred,
> That my body shuld be sold / my bloode be spylt so red;
> This [co]rs gravyn ded and cold / the thrid day ryse fro ded?
>
> (132–39)

With the addition of this invitation, the dramatist has invested
the meal with the significance of a communion. The first two
lines demand particular attention. The phrase "ettys for charite"
implies that to participate in communion is to express one's love
for God. Thus, the reciprocation of love for which Jesus repeatedly asks in the *Resurreccio* is here directly connected with the
sacramental observance. The Apostles are enjoined to eat that
their charity may be expressed in the action. Further, at line 133,
the charity *conferred in* communion is to be activated. Jesus' "I
ette at my fader will" probably derives from John 4:34: "Jesus
said to them, 'My food is to do the will of him who sent me, and
to accomplish his work.'" The Apostles, then, are to "ette" likewise that they may accomplish, through the charity bestowed in
communion, Jesus' work.

The significance of the ensuing lines is best understood in
comparison with the Gospel source. In Luke 24:44, after eating,
Jesus says to the Apostles, "'These are my words which I spoke
to you, while I was still with you, that everything written about
me in the law of Moses and the prophets and the psalms must be
fulfilled.'" In the play, Jesus uses the verb to "ette" to connect
communion with this redemptive fulfillment. As though further
to underline the speech's Eucharistic reference, the playwright
substitutes for the biblical "while I was still with you" the phrase
"in certan tyme and sted, / When I gaf myself to wold / to you in
fourme of bred." The institution is invoked as a signal that not
only Jesus' words but also his sacramental actions of the earlier
episode are being repeated and elucidated.

The remainder of the play is devoted to the incredulity of Thomas. The dramatic technique here employed recalls that of the *Mactacio Abel*. Thomas, like Cain, is initially characterized to attract sympathetic identification. Like Abel, the Apostles may at first be perceived as tediously preachy. In both plays, however, the evolving characterizations coupled with the audience's pre-existing religious knowledge enforce a shift of sympathy. The spectators withdraw their sympathy from the sinful, if initially attractive, characters and extend it toward the characters who stand for and speak the truth. The audience's final theologically correct response is the stronger for its having been arrived at through exploration and rejection of incorrect alternatives.

Initially, Thomas is spiritually comparable to the medieval Christian in the audience. He has missed Jesus' post-Resurrection appearances and so is required to accept on faith alone that the Resurrection has taken place. His first phrase, "If that I prowde as pacok go," suggests that he is costumed as a contemporary gallant, as do later references to his "hat," "mantill," "gyrdill gay," "purs of sylk," and "cote" (324, 332). This costuming and the sincere sorrow expressed in his speech render Thomas both accessible and sympathetic to members of the audience. His incredulity in the face of the Apostles' assertions will not at first shake that sympathy. The spectators are well aware that faith—particularly faith in the unseen—is no easy matter.

The Apostles argue at length with Thomas in the effort to convince him. Their sequential speeches serve more than one purpose. Not only do they communicate points of doctrine; they also dramatically represent the effects of communion. Like Luke and Cleophas at the close of the *Peregrini*, the Apostles are acting out the charity conferred by communion. They are certainly concerned with the expression of doctrinal truth, but even greater is their concern for their brother's spiritual welfare.

lefe thomas, flyte no more / bot trow and turne thi red.

(244)

Thyne hard hart this saull will dwyrd / Thomas, bot if thou blyn.

(252)

Thomas, brothere, turne thi thought / and trust that I say the.

(268)

That must thou nedelyngys trow / if thou thi saull will saue.

(272)

In their effort to convince Thomas and point him toward salvation, they realize for the audience the charity bestowed in the
communion meal.

That they fail in their effort is no reflection on the Apostles.
The dramatic technique enables the audience to be convinced—
or fortified in their existing conviction—despite Thomas's recalcitrance. At first Thomas's responses are designed to evoke the
audience's sympathy. Thomas speaks as much of his profound
grief as of his doubt.

> ffor his deth I am not glad / for sorow my hart will breke.
>
> (185)

> he luffyd vs well and faythfully / therfor sloes sorow me.
>
> (195)

> His dede me bryngys in great mowrneyng / and I withoutten red.
>
> (211)

But Thomas is not precisely "withoutten red," as the audience
perceives, and his ensuing speeches display more and more
querulousness and quibbling. His sorrow apparently forgotten,
he insistently sets up his "reason" against that of the Apostles,
perhaps invoking, to sensitized spectators, if not Lollardy's Scholastic breeding ground at least its characteristic contentiousness.

> All sam to me ye flyte / youre resons fast ye shawe,
> Bot tell me a skylle perfyte / any of you on raw.
>
> (216–17)

> Waloway! ye can no good / youre resons ar defaced,
> ye ar as women rad for blood / and lightly oft solaced.
>
> (232–33)

> lo, sich foly with you is / wysemen that shuld be,
> That thus a womans witnes trowys / better than ye se!
> In all youre skylles more and les / for mysfowndyng fayll ye;
> Might I se ihesu gost and flesh / gropyng shuld not gab me.
>
> (240–43)

Thomas's repeated assertion that he will not believe until he has
touched the wounds has an increasingly "janglyng" and blasphemous quality. His is not now the hyperbole of sorrow, but that
of stubborn, heretical self-proclaimed logic. The longer he persists in his "hardnes" (301), the less sympathy he will receive.

The audience's growing impatience with Thomas will find its relief in their shift of sympathy to the hardworking Apostles. This episode is not, as Prosser asserts, redundant, nor has "the whole point about the incredulity of Thomas . . . been destroyed"[28] by the prior depiction of the other Apostles' incredulity. Rather, the episode has allowed the spectators to work through and reject Thomas's dangerously attractive heretical lack of faith. They have found that they themselves know better than Thomas: they can accept—indeed, have accepted—invisible truth without ocular proof. When Jesus appears he pardons Thomas, and his final lines leave the audience justified in and rewarded for their superior faith.

> Thomas, for thou felys me / and my woundes bare,
> Mi risyng is trowed in the / and so was it not are;
> All that it trowes and not se / and dos after my lare,
> Euer blissid mot thay be / and heuen be theym yare!

(352–55)

Those later Christians, the audience included, believe without seeing. They have apprehended in the Eucharistic celebration the invisible Presence and have been, like the Apostles, spiritually strengthened by communion.

The succeeding play is the *Ascencio Domini*. This play incorporates into the cycle the scriptural accounts of Christ's final appearances to the Apostles, his commissioning of them to preach the Gospel, and his Ascension.[29] Further, the play is an effective sequel to the *Thomas Indie*, evidencing its link with the prior play in the evolving role of Thomas. It also anticipates the remainder of the cycle. The prominent role of Mary in the latter part of the episode prepares the audience for the subsequent plays, deleted by Reformation zeal from the Towneley manuscript, which are most likely to have comprised *The Descent of the Holy Spirit*, *The Death of Mary*, *The Appearance of Our Lady to Thomas*, and *The Assumption and Coronation of the Virgin*.[30] Finally, the *Ascencio* looks forward to the cycle's final play, the *Iudicium*. It is in Thomas's role and in eschatological anticipation that this play reflects continuing concern with Eucharistic doctrine.

Meyers notes that the "*Ascencio Domini* opens with a speech by Thomas, who is apparently given a part of importance only to join this pageant to the preceding one."[31] He goes on to suggest that Thomas is a comic figure in this play, providing "comic relief"[32] from the play's didacticism. In fact, the link between the two plays resides not simply in the continuity of character; it is also a doctrinal link. And if Thomas's role in the *Ascencio* is comic, it is not so much because he provides comic relief as because he unveils to the audience a visual, theologically decorous joke about the Mass.

Thomas's opening speech recalls to the audience the powerful resolution of the Apostles' doubts in the preceding play.

> Brethere all, that now here bene,
>   fforget my lorde yit may I nought;
> I wote not what it may mene,
>   Bot more I Weyn ther will be wrought.

$$(1-4)$$

The peevish recalcitrance that had cost him the audience's sympathy has been dissolved in his self-abasement and contrition at the end of the *Thomas Indie*. He is a renewed man at the beginning of the new play and once again commands sympathy. In fact, he has become a familiar traditional and literary type: from Mary Magdalen to Lancelot and beyond, the most attractive of Christian heroes are repentant sinners, and the Church always stands ready to embrace them, even when they are recanters of heresy. Thomas cannot forget his Lord, nor can he forget the lesson he has learned. In the place of the heretical logician stands an exemplary Apostle who, humbly admitting his ignorance of what is to come, is yet prepared for further wonders.

His anticipation is fulfilled. Jesus appears briefly (25–52) to foretell the descent of the Holy Spirit as well as his own reappearance. Thomas remains exemplary in his response. In a speech closely parallel to preceding speeches by Peter and Andrew he expresses an appropriate mixture of sorrow and joy.

> lang ore he saide, full openly,
>   that he must nedys fro vs twyn,
> And to his fader go in hy,
>   to Ioy of heuen that neuer shall blyn;
> Therefore we mowrne, both more and myn,
>   And mery also yit may we be.

$$(77-82)$$

Jesus reappears to comfort and commission the Apostles and again disappears. Peter, Andrew, and James express sorrow and fear at his absence, while John voices faith in Jesus' return. Then Thomas takes his turn.

> Of this carpyng now no more,
>   It drawes nygh the tyme of day;
> At oure mette I wold we wore,
>   he sende vs socowre that best may.

                                                    (178–81)

Meyers cites these lines as an indication that Thomas's role is
intended to be comic.[33] While it may be amusing to the spectator
that Thomas can think about supper at a moment like this, his
response is as theologically correct as John's and far more so than
those of Peter, Andrew, and James. Those Apostles' excessive
mourning and fear bespeak weak faith; Thomas's let's-get-on-
with-it attitude is that of a firm believer.

It is thirteen lines later that Jesus, having reappeared, speaks to
the group once again. It is tempting to speculate on the staging of
this episode, which might have been presented such that
Thomas's reference to "mette," functioning as a Eucharistic joke,
appeared to invoke Jesus. That is, Jesus might have appeared at or
shortly after the mention of "mette," visible to the audience, but
unnoticed by the other characters until he spoke. One imagines
the details of such a staging: during his speech, Thomas is
spreading a cloth on a table to the rear of the stage. He places on
it a loaf and perhaps some wine. Jesus' appearance behind the
table—easily managed by the actor—completes the icon, trans-
forming table into altar, meal into Mass.

Independent of this admittedly fanciful speculation, the proximity of Jesus' appearance to the cited lines suggests Eucharistic
allusion in "at oure mette I wold we wore." The exemplary
Thomas suggests—perhaps comically unwittingly—the celebration of a Mass, the invocation of the Real Presence, as a way of
coping with Jesus' frightening absence. The joke functions
within a context of Eucharistic orthodoxy. A reading for Corpus
Christi describes the Eucharist as not only a memorial of the
Passion, a fulfillment of figures, and the greatest of Christ's miracles, but also as "the unique solace of His saddening absence."[34]

At this point in the cycle, the sacrificial nature of the Eucharist, the doctrines of transubstantiation and the Real Presence, and the immediate effects of communion have all been
presented in forceful dramatic images. Only the sacrament's eschatological meaning has not yet been dramatically embodied.
The depiction of the Last Judgment is an essential completion of
the dramatic expression of orthodox Eucharistic doctrine. In the
Iudicium, those who have received the sacrament "in rightwys

lyfe" and who have been infused thereby with charity are granted their eternal reward. Those who have received it "in syn or stryfe," the uncharitable, and those who have denied its efficacy, are consigned to eager demons.

The Last Day, portrayed in the *Iudicium*, is anticipated in the earlier plays. Thus, the spectators' awareness of Last Things cannot lapse while other narrative and doctrinal concerns occupy the foreground. The depiction of the Judgment, of course, completes the audience's understanding of salvific history as a whole, not of the Eucharist alone. Anticipations of final Judgment in these earlier plays are, however, especially important to the cycle's sacramental focus.

Eschatological anticipation is first evident in this group of plays at the end of the *Thomas Indie*. Having proved his own Resurrection to Thomas by appearing before him, Jesus speaks of the resurrection of all "on domesday."

> Who so hath not trowid right / to hell I shall theym lede,
> Ther euer more is dark as nyght / and greatt paynes to drede;
> Those that trow in my myght / and luf well almus dede,
> Thai shall shyne as son bright / and heuen haue to thare mede.
>
> (344–47)

This stanza describes the fate of those who have not "trowid right": although Thomas is forgiven, damnation awaits others who—like the Lollards—for lack of ocular proof persistently refuse to believe in the mysteries of the faith. The saved, on the other hand, are characterized as charitable as well as faithful. They are those who, like Thomas's brother Apostles, have enjoyed the special benefits of communion.

In the *Ascencio* eschatological anticipation becomes a thematic concern in its own right. Aware that Jesus is soon to ascend to his Father, the Apostles quite naturally begin to think of his return at the Second Coming. As Philip puts it,

> We may mowrne, no meruell why / for we oure master thus shall mys,
> That shall go fro vs sodanly / and we ne wote what cause is,
> Neuer the les the sothe is this / he saide that he shuld com agane
> To bryng vs all to blys / therof may we be fane.
>
> (95–98)

The powerful consolation of the promised Second Coming is also evidenced in the attending angels' speeches.

> . . . as ye sagh hym sty
> Into heuen on hy,
> In flesh and fell in his body
>   ffrom erthe now here,
> Right so shall he, securly,
> com downe agane truly,
> with his woundys blody,
>   To deme you all in fere.
>
> (262–69)

> Who so his byddyng will obey,
>   And thare mys amende,
> With hym shall haue blys on hy,
>   And won ther withoutten ende,
>
> And who that wyrk amys,
>   And theym amende will neuer,
> Shall neuer com in heuen blys,
>   Bot to hell banyshed for euer.
>
> (290–97)

None of the Apostles and few among the spectators are likely to have identified themselves with this second group. The cycle's penultimate play leaves the audience fortified, in knowledge and faith, against such a fate. They arrive at the brink of the Judgment play with a clear sense of how they may participate in salvation through the teachings and rituals of the orthodox Church and, one may imagine, an eager hunger to do so.

8
Conclusion: The Last Mass

Rosemary Woolf has argued that "the Last Judgment is a penitential theme which arouses fear not delight."[1] Corpus Christi is a festival of joy, and in Woolf's view a Last Judgment play is therefore not an apt conclusion to a Corpus Christi cycle. As I have suggested, however, in discussion of the plays leading up to the Towneley *Iudicium*, the Last Day may also be joyfully anticipated as the moment of final reunion with Christ. The *Iudicium*, in its cyclical context, is as appropriate to the celebration of the Corpus Christi occasion as is a play of the Resurrection or the Last Supper. Only in a play depicting the joyfully awaited day of Judgment can the spectator witness a dramatic embodiment of Jesus' final direct words about the Eucharist to the audience: "Whoso it takys in rightwys lyfe / Dy shall he neuer." The *Iudicium* effectively combines the directly sacramental theme initiated in the *Resurreccio* with the effectively counter-Lollard themes of use and abuse of language that permeate the cycle. This combination is largely the result of interpolations by the Wakefield Master into a play borrowed from York.[2] As such, it suggests how the cycles may have been progressively transmuted, through successive revisions, to remain responsive to current conditions and the religious educational needs of the lay audience.

The opening of the *Iudicium* is lost. The extant portion opens upon the discussion of a group of evil souls on their way to Judgment. The souls are filled with dread, and the focus of that dread, significantly, is the anticipated *sight* of their Lord.

> Alas, that I was borne!
> I se now me beforne,
>   That lord with Woundys fyfe;
> how may I on hym loke,
> That falsly hym forsoke,
>   When I led synfull lyfe?

                                                    (11–16)

What this soul is anticipating does occur in the Judgment scene at the play's dramatic center. In that scene, Jesus stands before the assembled souls, good and evil, and "*ostendit eis Wlnera sua* [shows them his wounds]" (stage direction following 401).

> here may ye se my Woundys wide
>   that I suffred for youre mysdede,
> Thrugh harte, hede, fote, hande and syde,
>   not for my gilte bot for youre nede.
> Behold both bak, body. and syde,
>   how dere I boght youre broder-hede,
> Thise bitter paynes I wold abide,
>   to by you blys thus wold I blede.
>
>   (402–9)

The scene presents a dramatically powerful icon: Christ in the form of the Image of Pity.[3] It visually duplicates and forcefully recalls the scene of Christ's monologue in the *Resurreccio*. The bleeding body was there defined as a sacrifice, the salvific effect of which is perpetuated in the Mass of "brede, myn awne body" (*Resurreccio*, 327). The familiar artistic motif of the Image of Pity has thus become a Eucharistic symbol. As J. W. Robinson suggests, "It is perhaps significant that many of the Guilds of Corpus Christi had in their chapels Images of Pity."[4] The use of this image as the focus of the Judgment scene makes dramatically evident the connection between the sacrament and its eschatological effects. Clifford Davidson describes the impact of the Image of Pity on the souls and, indirectly, upon the spectators.

> Christ has literally given his body for mankind; he is the living bread which, the sequence for Corpus Christi warns us, must give us strength if we are not to die. To the blessed at the Judgment, the sight of the actual wounds of their Lord is the consummation of the vision of his mercy which previously in this life had only been present in the Eucharistic ritual. To the damned souls arrayed at the Judge's left hand, however, the wounds are no longer symbols of Mercy, for they have rejected the body of Christ. . . . His wounds reproach and judge those who have chosen the way of perversity.[5]

The reproach would be especially sharp to the Lollard, whose "perversity" has barred him or her from Eucharistic piety.

The Image of Pity, in the *Resurreccio* and *Iudicium* monologues, becomes a speaking icon, the Word as sacrament, with both scenes functioning as, one might say, hyper-Masses. The dramatic action surrounding this icon reveals the ways in which individuals' uses of language reflect their eternal relationship to the divine Word manifested in the Eucharist. While this concern is present in the earlier strata of the *Iudicium*, it is brilliantly sharpened in the Wakefield Master's interpolations.

Prominent among the regrets of the damned souls is their past abuse of language: "That I wold fayne were hyd / my synfull wordys and vayn, / fful new now mon be rekynyd / vp to me agayn" (47–48). But there is nothing the souls can say to the Judge to undo their wickedness. The final inefficacy of evil—including, of course, heretical—language is revealed in a new and terrifying light: "Where I was wonte to go / and haue my Wordys at will, / Now am I set full thro / and fayn to hold me still" (65–66). The evil souls have at last recognized the wickedness of their "janglyng" and the inevitability that God's Word will prevail.

The first Wakefield Master interpolation begins at line 89. Here enters a group of "janglyng" demons, hurrying to give evidence against the damned souls. Of the sins specified, the majority involve abuse of language.

> here is a bag full, lokys,
>   of pride and of lust,
> Of Wraggers and wrears / a bag full of brefes,
> Of carpars and cryars / of mychers and thefes,
> Of lurdans and lyars / that no man lefys,
> Of flytars, of flyars / and renderars of reffys.

> (141–46)

Among the sinners are those who are guilty of verbal duplicity—"before hym he prase hym, / behynde he mys-sase hym" (157–58)—and those "dere darlyngys" of Pilate's, the "bakbytars" and "fals quest-dytars" (184, 185). The dramatist may have found suggestion or warrant for this focus in the writings of another Yorkshireman, Richard Rolle (d. 1349), who stresses in *The Pricke of Conscience* that, at Judgment, account must be made of every moment of life, including every word and thought.

> *De omni verbo ociosi in die iudicii*
> *reddenda est racio.*
> Þe buke says shortly on þis manere:
> "Of ilkan idel word and vayne here,
> Reson sal be yholder right
> At þe day of dome, in Goddes sight;"

> And noght anely of idel wordes sayd,
> Bot of ilk idel thoght þat God noght payd.[6]

The notion that verbal misbehavior will come under scrutiny on Judgment Day is not the playwright's invention. However, as this notion functions in the play, it contributes to the cycle's potential counter-Lollardy. The play's thematic focus upon abuse of language is sharpened still further at the demon Tutivillus's entrance. Tutivillus traditionally has jurisdiction over "kyrk-chaterars," those who gossip during Mass, but, as Davidson puts it, the demon in this play "has expanded duties."[7] Davidson notes that the demon's usual motto, "*Fragmina psalmorum colligit horum,*" is modified by the stage Tutivillus: "*verborum*" takes the place of "*psalmorum,*"[8] indicating the demon's interest in all forms of linguistic abuse. Tutivillus, most strikingly, asserts, "Now am I master lollar, / And of sich men I mell me" (213–14). Margaret Jennings argues that the playwright's reference is probably not to Lollards but to mumbling "idlers," those who are too lazy to say their prayers properly.[9] But in the climate in which the plays first appeared, it is unlikely that this reference failed to connote Lollardy.[10] A devil's claiming to be the "master" of all Lollards is in keeping with the persistent anti-Lollard tradition of viewing John Wyclif as the devil or the devil's henchman. Tutivillus's remark serves to highlight Lollards among other abusers of language in the same way that the cycle as a whole makes this connection.

Tutivillus himself is a "jangler," practicing what he preaches against. Even his infernal colleagues complain, "with wordes will thou fill vs" (247). He is well qualified to recognize and round up "janglyng" sinners: "fals swearars" (279), "kyrk-chaterars" (296), and "runkers and rowners" (298). Abusers of language are prominent among those he welcomes to hell.

> ye lurdans and lyars / mychars and thefes,
> fflytars and flyars / that all men reprefes,
> Spolars, extorcyonars / Welcom, my lefes!
> ffals Iurars and vsurars / to symony that clevys,
>   To tell;
> hasardars and dysars,
> ffals dedys forgars,
> Slanderars, bakbytars,
>   All vnto hell.

> (359–67)

The "janglyng" in hell—the demons' own and their references to the sinners' verbal faults—provides a contrast that enhances the effect of the solemn Judgment scene and the force of the words of Judgment.[11]

The efficacy of God's Word is demonstrated in the Judgment scene. As in the case of the Creation monologue, the Word effects what it expresses. Again, the cycle dramatists are not the first to have implied such a comparison. Rolle, for example, remarking on how quickly judgment is effected, goes on to make this connection:

> Also grete a wonder es when he wroght,
> With a short worde, alle þe world of noght,
> And of þis þe prophete bers wittnes,
> Þat says þus, als it wryten es:
> Quia ipse dixit et facta sunt,
> ipse mandavit et creata sunt.
> "God sayde," says he, "and alle was done
> He bad and alle was made sone."[12]

None but verbal action is required to realize the salvation of the good and the damnation of the evil. The eschatological message to the audience is powerful. Here, at last, at the last Mass of human history, the audience sees the meaning of Christ's words about the Eucharist.

> who so it resaues in syn or stryfe
>   Bese ded for euer;
> And whoso it takys in rightwys lyfe
>   Dy shall he neuer.
>
> (Resurreccio, 330–33)

The closing passage of the Iudicium serves to characterize more fully these eternal states. A second Wakefield Master interpolation reintroduces the "janglyng" demons, driving before them the damned souls who now "be dom / somtyme were full melland" (595). The enemies of God's Word are now mute. The Word's servants and vehicles have the last word in a speech that significantly echoes that of the Cherubim in the Creation play.

> We loue the, lorde, in alkyn thyng,
>   That for thyne awne has ordand thus,
> That we may haue now oure dwellyng

In heuen blis giffen vnto vs.
Therfor full boldly may we syng
On oure way as we trus;
Make we all myrth and louyng
With te deum laudamus.

(613–20)

Silence follows. The cycle is complete.

*   *   *

Eucharistic reference thematically and stylistically unifies the
Towneley cycle and makes of it a bastion for orthodoxy replete
with counter-Lollard force. The theme of God's Word and humanity's response to it makes of the drama a continuous history
culminating in the institution and elucidation of the Eucharist.
The sacrament is itself a powerful manifestation of God's Word in
extrabiblical form. On the basis of this equation, the cycle becomes an effective apologia for precisely those orthodox beliefs
that the Lollards most frequently called into question. Simultaneously it provides the audience with a version of the "Englished
Bible" the lay hunger for which the Lollards had also recognized
and tried to appease.

The cycle's Old Testament plays trace the earliest interventions
of God's Word into human history. God's Word effects Creation;
subsequently it is addressed to the patriarchs, guiding their actions and shaping their experiences. The continuum of God's
Word from the time of Moses to that of its Incarnation is reflected
in the sequence of speeches constituting the *Processus prophetarum*.

The good characters' response to God's Word from the cycle's
earliest plays provides a model for the spectators' religious response. Repeatedly, the dramatized responses evoke the audience's liturgical experience. The good angels praise their
Creator with a phrase from the *Pater Noster*; Abel offers a sacrifice foreshadowing the sacrifice of the Mass; Jacob builds and
consecrates the first "kyrk." Throughout, the biblical exemplars
are priestlike in words and actions, and they reinforce the spectators' respectful awe for priesthood and ritual. Contrastingly, the
"janglyng" language of the evil characters is presented as a negative example. Evil is defined as heretical enmity to God's Word,
often with a specifically Lollard cast. Debate expresses the strife
of good and evil, orthodoxy and heresy. Also introduced is the
notion that hunger signals a character's distance from God. Cut
off from the "gostly fode" of God's Word, characters like Cain's

Garcio and Noah's Uxor experience what they define as physical hunger. As the cycle unfolds, the audience recognizes the spiritual dimension of that hunger and its Eucharistic remedy.

In the cycle's central group of plays, the Word is manifested as Christ, the Word Incarnate. God's Word brought to the patriarchs the law and prophecies of salvation; the Word Incarnate fulfills the law and realizes humanity's redemption. The plays depicting Christ's life insistently point ahead to the Passion and death, the Resurrection, and the enduring sacramental Presence of the Word. The audience's liturgical experience remains focal. Their experience of the Eucharist—particularly at the highly charged moment of its elevation—is recurrently evoked through striking dramatic embodiment. The evil characters continue to "jangle" their challenges to orthodoxy; the good continue to use language economically, truthfully, often sacerdotally. References to hunger and food accumulate, contributing to the cycle's increasingly sharp focus on the Eucharist. In the Passion sequence, the very action commemorated and revivified in the sacrament is depicted. Here, the Word Incarnate encounters and vanquishes his enemies. He speaks little. It is his quiet presence—identical with the sacramental Presence—that achieves the victory. The counter-Lollard force of these central plays has less and less to do with negative images of heresy, more and more with positive images of the sacrament. In the cycle's final group of plays, positive counter-Lollardy continues to operate as the Eucharist is most directly considered. The postponement of the sacramental institution until the moment of the Resurrection allows for the creation of a striking dramatic icon. Christ, newly risen, speaks of the sacrament; the spectators, prepared by their liturgical experience, perceive a speaking sacrament, the sacramental fulfillment of God's Word. The equation is complete and provides a stunning answer to Lollards, who belittled the sacrament and sought God's Word in scriptura sola. Christ's post-Resurrection appearances to the Apostles, similarly, are depicted in liturgical terms, as if in response to Lollard denial that Christ ordained the Mass rituals. The meaning of the sacrament to the communicant is also explored through dramatic embodiment. Protocommunicants like Luke and Cleophas are immediately affected and motivated to virtuous action. The sacrament's eschatological meaning to the communicant is focal in the *Iudicium*, where, too, the cycle's theme of use and abuse of language is brought to culmination.

The Wakefield Master's contributions to the Towneley cycle significantly enhance existing Eucharistic focus in the plays. In his work—including additions to the *Mactacio Abel* and the *Iudicium* and, in their entirety, the *Noe*, the two shepherds' plays, the *Herod*, and the *Coliphizacio*—he extends the cycle's use of the audience's liturgical experience, and he sharpens focus on the proper use and abuse of language. His work appears to reflect a heightened concern with Eucharistic themes at a time when Lollardy, creeping northward, assailed both sacrament and priesthood. Whatever his intention, the Towneley cycle he completed, like the Feast of Corpus Christi itself, is a brilliant celebration of the Eucharist. The celebration had the power and energy to strengthen orthodoxy and—when the necessity arose—to combat the sacrament's heretical detractors.

Notes

Introduction

1. There is considerable consensus that this cycle was played at Wakefield. My use of the name *Towneley*, derived from an early owner of the manuscript, is not intended to cast doubt on this probability.

2. David Mills, " 'The Towneley Plays' or 'The Towneley Cycle'?" *Leeds Studies in English*, n.s., 17 (1986): 96.

3. For some recent discussion concerning the dangers and values of critical concentration on doctrinal matters in the cycles, see Albert H. Tricomi, ed., *Early Drama to 1600*, Acta (Proceedings of SUNY Regional Conference in Medieval Studies), vol. 13 (Binghamton: Center for Medieval and Early Renaissance Studies, State University of New York at Binghamton, 1987). Tricomi cautions against the procrustean interpretation of "entire cycles . . . as unified, doctrinal expressions of a communal mentality" ("Critical Introduction,' iv). In "The Texts of Civic Religious Drama: Collections of Anthologies," in the same volume, Stanley J. Kahrl allows that "thematic studies are an important mode of seeing; they enrich our understanding, but they run the risk of becoming reductive" (65). I acknowledge that risk but consider it worth taking in the pursuit of a "mode of seeing" that merits exploration.

4. I will discuss DeWelles's views further in chap. 6.

5. Russell Fraser, *The War against Poetry* (Princeton: Princeton University Press, 1970); Jonas Barish, *The Antitheatrical Prejudice* (Berkeley: University of California Press, 1981).

6. Fraser, *War against Poetry*, 28, 43.

7. Barish, *Antitheatrical Prejudice*, 58.

8. Ibid., 67, 69. On the *Tretise's* relationship to Tertullian's *De Spectaculis* and later antitheatrical documents, see also Clifford Davidson's introduction to his edition of the tract: *A Middle English Treatise on the Playing of Miracles* (Washington, D.C.: University Press of America, 1981), 3–8.

9. Barish, *Antitheatrical Prejudice*, 71, and see 76.

10. Ritchie D. Kendall, *The Drama of Dissent: The Radical Poetics of Non-conformity, 1380–1590* (Chapel Hill: University of North Carolina Press, 1986).

11. Ibid., 7, 50, 16.

12. Ibid., 17, 20. See also Davidson, introduction to *Middle English Treatise*, 16: "The concept of the divine *Logos* as potentially communicated through the sense of sight by way of an image . . . is rejected [by the Lollards] in favor of communication through language alone whenever possible."

13. Kendall, *Drama of Dissent*, 51.

Chapter 1. Lollardy and Drama

1. See Harold C. Gardiner, *Mysteries' End* (1946; reprint, Hamden, Conn.: Archon, 1967). Gardiner's book demonstrates that the Corpus Christi plays were

146 Notes

seen during the Reformation as a powerful and dangerous embodiment of "papistry" and that the stage was drawn into the polemical service of both theologies; see especially 58–63. See also Bing D. Bitts, "The 'Suppression Theory' and the English Corpus Christi Play: A Re-Examination," *Theatre Journal* 32 (1980): 157–68. Bitts suggests that Gardiner's "suppression theory" is liable to oversimplification but concedes that suppression did indeed take place.

2. On the dating of the cycles, see, for example, E. K. Chambers, *The Medieval Stage* (London: Oxford University Press, 1903), 2:109; David Bevington, *Medieval Drama* (Boston: Houghton Mifflin, 1975), 227–35; Richard Beadle, ed., *The York Plays* (London: Edward Arnold, 1982), 19–23. Martin Stevens, in *Four Middle English Mystery Cycles: Textual, Contextual, and Critical Interpretations* (Princeton: Princeton University Press, 1987), would date the Towneley cycle later—"some time in the last third of the fifteenth century" (118). While such a date would make the cycle a belated response to Lollardy, it would not preclude my hypothesis. On the contrary, a late fifteenth-century cycle could well have served as a response to the Lollardy that (as I will discuss in this chapter) was itself a late phenomenon in the north.

3. George Macaulay Trevelyan, *England in the Age of Wycliffe, 1368–1520* (1899; reprint, New York: Harper & Row, 1963), 293.

4. See "Sixteen Points on which the Bishops accuse Lollards" and "Twelve Conclusions of the Lollards," in Anne Hudson, ed., *Selections from English Wycliffite Writings* (Cambridge: Cambridge University Press, 1978), 19–29; see also Norman P. Tanner, ed., *Heresy Trials in the Diocese of Norwich, 1428–31*, Camden Fourth Series, vol. 20 (London: Royal Historical Society, 1977), 11–12, 57, 111.

5. Trevelyan, *Age of Wycliffe*, map following 352.

6. A. G. Dickens, *Lollards and Protestants in the Diocese of York, 1509–1558* (London and New York: published for the University of Hull by the Oxford University Press, 1959).

7. Current research suggests that there were relative few cycle plays. Such a list as that provided in A. C. Cawley et al., eds., *The Revels History of Drama in English*, Volume I: *Medieval Drama* (London: Methuen, 1983), 293–302— "Manuscripts and Contents of the Extant English Cycles"—is likely, therefore, to be geographically representative. The Chester, Towneley (Wakefield), and York cycles are northern; Beverley, Yorkshire, also appears to have had a complete cycle: see V. A. Kolve, *The Play Called Corpus Christi* (Stanford, Calif.: Stanford University Press, 1966), 50. Biblical plays surviving from other parts of the country may or may not have belonged to analogous cycles.

8. John A. F. Thomson, *The Later Lollards, 1414–1520* (London: Oxford University Press, 1965), 192–201. See also Anne Hudson, *The Premature Reformation: Wycliffite Texts and Lollard History* (Oxford: Clarendon Press, 1988), 126–27.

9. Charles Kightly, "The Early Lollards: A Survey of Popular Lollard Activity in England, 1382–1428" (Ph.D. diss., University of York, 1975), chap. 1.

10. James Edward McGoldrick, "Patrick Hamilton, Luther's Scottish Disciple," *The Sixteenth Century Journal* 18 (1987): 81–82.

11. Thomson, *Later Lollards*, 197.

12. Ibid., 200.

13. Ibid., 195.

14. See Mak's impersonation of a southern yeoman and the shepherds' hostile response: *Secunda Pastorum*, 201–16, in George England and Alfred W. Pollard, eds., *The Towneley Plays*, Early English Text Society (1897; reprint, Millwood, N.Y.: Kraus, 1978). All references to the Towneley plays are based on this edition. The action of the fourteenth-century *Sir Gawain and the Green Knight* depicts similar regional sentiments, as I discuss in "The Contrasted Courts in *Sir Gawain and the Green Knight*," in *The Medieval Court in Europe*, ed. Edward R. Haymes, Houston German Studies 6 (Munich: Wilhelm Fink Verlag, 1986), 200–208.

15. Hudson, *Selections*, 25.

16. Thomas Netter [?], *Fasciculi Zizaniorum Magistri Johannis Wyclif Cum Tritico*, ed. Walter Waddington Shirley (London: Longman, Brown, Green, Longmans, and Roberts, 1858), 296–307.

17. James Gairdner, *Lollardy and the Reformation in England: An Historical Survey* (New York: Burt Franklin, 1908), 1:126.

18. Herbert B. Workman, *John Wyclif: A Study of the English Medieval Church* (1926; reprint, Hamden, Conn.: Archon, 1966), 2:17, 101.

19. "Images and Pilgrimages," in Hudson, *Selections*, 83.

20. W. R. Jones, "Lollards and Images: The Defense of Religious Art in Later Medieval England," *Journal of the History of Ideas* 34 (1973): 32, 34, 35.

21. "De officio pastorali," in F. D. Matthew, ed., *The English Works of Wyclif Hitherto Unprinted*, Early English Text Society (London: Kegan Paul, Trench, Trübner, 1880), 438.

22. "Sermon CXXXIX," in Thomas Arnold, ed., *Select English Works of John Wyclif* (Oxford: The Clarendon Press, 1869), 1:216. It must here be pointed out that a four-volume collection, *English Wycliffite Sermons*, is in preparation: vols. 1, edited by Anne Hudson (Oxford: Clarendon Press, 1983), and 2, edited by Pamela Gradon (1988) have thus far appeared. Vol. 4, which will include discussion of the sermons' authorship, will likely correct some earlier misattributions of sermons to Wyclif himself.

23. "Of Feigned Contemplative Life," in Matthew, *English Works of Wyclif*, 191.

24. Kendall, *Drama of Dissent*, 28.

25. Herbert E. Winn, ed., *Wyclif: Selected English Writings* (1929; reprint, New York: AMS Press, 1976), 104–5.

26. "De officio pastorali," in Matthew, *English Works of Wyclif*, 429.

27. Arnold, *Select English Works* 1:250. "Plaies," of course, need not refer to Corpus Christi plays or even specifically to drama at all.

28. "The Ave Maria," in Matthew, *English Works of Wyclif*, 206.

29. J. S. Brewer, ed., *Monumenta Franciscana* (London: Longman, Brown, Green, Longmans, and Roberts, 1858), 607.

30. See Kolve, *Play Called Corpus Christi*, 282n.82.

31. Brewer, *Monumenta Franciscana*, 607.

32. Davidson, *Middle English Treatise*.

33. Ibid., 38.

34. Ibid., 52. On both the poem and the *Tretise*, see also Kendall, *Drama of Dissent*, 53–54.

35. Cecilia Cutts, "The Croxton Play: An Anti-Lollard Piece," *Modern Language Quarterly* 5 (1944): 52. See also John Fines, "Studies in the Lollard Heresy. Being an Examination of the Evidence from the Dioceses of Norwich,

Lincoln, Coventry and Lichfield, and Ely, during the period 1430–1530" (Ph.D. diss., University of Sheffield, 1964), 41, 89, and 133. Fines cites anti-Lollard tracts and both university and ecclesiastical mandates for preaching, often for preaching in English.

36. Cutts, "The Croxton Play," 52–53.

37. Peter W. Travis, *Dramatic Design in the Chester Cycle* (Chicago: University of Chicago Press, 1982), 236–37.

38. See G. R. Owst, *Literature and Pulpit in Medieval England* (1933; reprint, New York: Barnes & Noble, 1966), 479–80; and Gardiner, *Mysteries' End*, 11.

39. Owst, *Literature and Pulpit*, 485. See also Davidson, introduction to *Middle English Treatise*, 17–19.

40. Francis Drake, *Eboracum; or, The History and Antiquities of the City of York* (London: William Bowyer, 1736), xxix.

41. David Mills, "The Drama of Religious Ceremony," in Cawley et al., *Revels History*, 208.

42. See James Hamilton Wylie, *History of England under Henry the Fourth* (London: Longmans, Green, 1896), 3:204–5.

43. Mervyn James, "Ritual, Drama and Social Body in the Late Medieval English Town," *Past and Present* 98 (February 1983): 3–29. See also Peter W. Travis, "The Social Body of the Dramatic Christ in Medieval England," in Tricomi, *Early Drama to 1600*, 17–36.

44. James, "Ritual, Drama and Social Body," 4, 9, 15.

45. Text in Bevington, *Medieval Drama*, 940–63.

46. Text in Norman Davis, ed., *Non-Cycle Plays and Fragments*, Early English Text Society (London: Oxford University Press, 1970), 58–89.

47. Cutts, "The Croxton Play," 47; see also Mills, "Drama and Folk Ritual," in Cawley et al., *Revels History*, 151.

48. Thomas Netter [Waldensis], *Doctrinale Antiquitatem Fidei Catholicae Ecclesiae. De Sacramentalibus* (1759; reprint, Plymouth, Mich.: Gregg Press, 1967), 3.36.

49. Bevington, *Medieval Drama*, 235.

50. Workman, *John Wyclif* 2:201.

Chapter 2. The Major Controversies: Theologies of the Word and the Sacrament

1. Arnold, *Select English Works* 2:169–70.

2. Hudson, *Selections*, 17.

3. See J. I. Catto, "John Wyclif and the Cult of the Eucharist," in *The Bible in the Medieval World: Essays in Memory of Beryl Smalley*, ed. Katherine Walsh and Diana Wood (Oxford: published for the Ecclesiastical History Society by Basil Blackwell, 1985), 269–86.

4. "Twelve Conclusions of the Lollards," in Hudson, *Selections*, 25.

5. Joseph Rawson Lumby, ed., *Chronicon Henrici Knighton* (London, 1889), 2:159.

6. See Michael Fox, "John Wyclif and the Mass," *Heythrop Journal* 3 (1962): 232–40; Workman, *John Wyclif* 2:36–40.

7. Woodburn O. Ross, ed., *Middle English Sermons*, Early English Text Society (London: Oxford University Press, 1960), 126–27.

8. John Mirk, *Mirk's Festial: A Collection of Homilies by Johannis Mirkus*

(John Mirk), ed. Theodore Erbe, Early English Text Society (London: Kegan Paul, Trench, Trübner, 1905), pt. 1, 168–75.

9. Alan J. Fletcher, "John Mirk and the Lollards," *Medium Aevum* 56 (1987): 218, 220.

10. Kendall, *Drama of Dissent*, 23, 32.

11. Trevelyan, *Age of Wyclif*, 128. See also Workman, *John Wyclif* 2:151; and Janel M. Mueller, *The Native Tongue and the Word: Developments in English Prose Style 1380–1580* (Chicago and London: University of Chicago Press, 1984), 43–45.

12. Workman, *John Wyclif* 2:209.

13. *Wycklyffes Wicket* (1546; reprint, Oxford: Oxford University Press, 1828), n.p. (sec. vii). See also Lilian M. Swinburn, ed. *The Lantern of Liʒt*, Early English Text Society (London: Kegan Paul, Trench, Trübner, 1917), 31–32.

14. Margaret Aston, *Lollards and Reformers: Images and Literacy in Late Medieval Religion* (London: The Hambledon Press, 1984), 130–31.

15. Ibid., 66.

16. Workman, *John Wyclif* 2:211, 149–50.

17. Arnold, *Select English Works* 2:1.

18. Wycliffite tract, "How men ought to obey prelates," in Matthew, *English Works of Wyclif*, 37–38. Lollard writings not only assert the falsehood of exegetical glosses but also argue—albeit disingenuously—that writers of such glosses must believe Scripture to be false without them: see Matthew, *English Works of Wyclif*, 266–67; Arnold, *Select English Works* 1:376.

19. Hudson, *Premature Reformation*, 248, 274–75. However, as Hudson points out, the compilers of the Lollard *Glossed Gospels* "apprehended the possibilities of the medium of derivative commentary for the demonstration of Wycliffite viewpoints" (258).

20. See Owst, *Literature and Pulpit*, 60–62, on the Benedictine Rypon's arguments against literalism.

21. Gairdner, *Lollardy and the Reformation* 1:189.

22. Ross, *Middle English Sermons*, 223.

23. Ibid., 13, 14.

24. Thomas Frederick Simmons, ed., *The Lay Folks Mass Book*, Early English Text Society (1879; reprint, London: Oxford University Press, 1968), 16, lines 160–68; 18, line 181.

25. Ibid., 140, lines 431–36.

26. Ibid., 140, lines 446–48.

27. Ibid., 379n.

28. Ibid., 146, lines 642–49.

29. Rev. Joseph A. Jungmann, *The Mass of the Roman Rite: Its Origins and Development (Missarum Sollemnia)* New York: Benziger Brothers, 1951), 2:447.

30. Jules Corblet, *Histoire dogmatique, liturgique et archéologique du sacrement de l'Eucharistie* (Paris: Société Générale de Librairie Catholique, 1885–86), 1:81, 94.

31. Ibid., 97. See also 91 and 105 for similar testimony from the writings of Irenaeus and Cyril of Alexandria.

32. From a commentary on Psalm 147 cited in Germain Morin, *Etudes, textes, découverts: contributions à la littérature et à l'histoire des douze premiers siècles* (Paris: A. Picard, 1913), 1:243–44. Here and hereafter, translations are mine unless otherwise noted.

33. Paschasius Radbertus, "De Corpore et Sanguine Domini," in *Patrologiae*

Cursus Completus: Series Latina, ed. J. P. Migne (Paris, 1852), vol. 120, col. 1272.

34. Ratramnus of Corbie, "De Corpore et Sanguine Domini," in Migne, *Patrologia Latina,* vol. 121, col. 145.

35. M.-D. Chenu, *Toward Understanding St. Thomas,* trans. A.-M. Landry and D. Hughes (Chicago: Henry Regnery, 1964), 308.

36. Saint Thomas Aquinas, *Summa Theologiae,* vol. 7, ed. and trans. T. C. O'Brien (New York: McGraw-Hill, 1976), 39, 1a34, 3.

37. *Summa Theologiae,* vol. 56, ed. and trans. David Bourke (1975), 2; Bourke's translation, 3.

38. Ibid., 21, 3a60, 6.

39. Bourke, "Introduction," in *Summa Theologiae,* vol. 56, xviii.

40. Francis Proctor and Christopher Wordsworth, eds., *Breviarum ad usum insignis ecclesiae Sarum* (Cambridge, 1882), vol. 1, col. 1064.

41. Ibid., cols. 1072–73.

42. Jerome Taylor, "The Dramatic Structure of the Middle English Corpus Christi, or Cycle, Plays," in *Medieval English Drama: Essays Critical and Contextual,* ed. Jerome Taylor and Alan H. Nelson (Chicago: University of Chicago Press, 1972), 150.

43. Ibid., 151.

44. Ibid., 150–51.

45. Proctor and Wordsworth, *Breviarum,* vol. 1, col. 1080.

46. Ibid., col. 1083. See also cols. 1082–82, 1088.

47. On the connection between the Septuagesima readings and the Old Testament incidents in the cycle, see James W. Earl, "The Shape of Old Testament History in the Towneley Plays," *Studies in Philology* 69 (1972): 434–52.

48. Jungmann, *Mass of the Roman Rite* 1:391. See also 393–403 on traditions concerning the choice of scriptural readings for Mass.

49. Ibid., 419–20.

50. Cited in T. E. Bridgett, *A History of the Holy Eucharist in Great Britain* (London: T. Fisher Unwin, 1908), 103.

51. Mabel Day, ed., *The English Text of the Ancrene Riwle,* Early English Text Society (London: Oxford University Press, 1952), 13–14.

52. Simmons, *Lay Folks Mass Book,* appendix 3, 122.

53. Ibid., 152.

54. Richard Leighton Greene, ed., *The Early English Carols* (Oxford: Clarendon Press, 1935), 229 (no. 334). See also 229–30 (no. 335).

55. Netter, *Doctrinale,* LVIII.6, col. 357. The translation is by Darwell Stone, in *A History of the Doctrine of the Holy Eucharist* (London: Longmans, Green, 1909), 379.

56. Stevens, *Four Middle English Mystery Cycles,* 191–92.

57. Margaret Deanesly, *The Lollard Bible and Other Medieval Biblical Versions* (Cambridge: Cambridge University Press, 1920), 321. See also Hudson, *Premature Reformation,* 437–40.

58. Deanesly, *Lollard Bible,* 323, 231.

59. See ibid., 323. See also Mueller, *Native Tongue,* 77–83.

60. Nicholas Love, trans., *The Mirrour of the Blessed Lyf of Jesu Christ,* ed. Lawrence F. Powell (Oxford: Clarendon Press, 1908), 320.

61. Ibid., 306.

62. Cutts, "The Croxton Play," 54.

63. Ibid., 55.

64. Lumby, *Chronicon* 2:163.

65. Translated by Workman in *John Wyclif* 2:272.

66. Kendall, *Drama of Dissent*, 51.

67. Travis, *Dramatic Design*, 5, 14.

68. Five complete plays—the *Processus Noe*, the *Prima* and the *Secunda Pastorum*, the *Magnus Herodes*, and the *Coliphizacio*—are conventionally attributed to the Wakefield Master, along with significant revisions of at least the *Mactacio Abel* and the *Iudicium*.

69. Stevens, *Four Middle English Mystery Cycles*, 117, 88–89. See also 120–21.

70. A. C. Cawley includes the *Mactacio Abel* in his *The Wakefield Pageants in the Towneley Cycle* (Manchester: Manchester University Press, 1958).

71. Stevens, *Four Middle English Mystery Cycles*, 127.

72. Travis, *Dramatic Design*, 23.

Chapter 3. The Case of Cain

1. Stevens, *Four Middle English Mystery Cycles*, 78. Stevens notes that critics have tended to focus "on the benefit that a view through the perspective of the present lent to the audience's perception of the past"; he argues that "the reverse view is equally possible and . . . enlightening. We can look by means of the anachronistic perspective through the past into the present."

2. R. T. Davies, ed., *Medieval English Lyrics* (Chicago: Northwestern University Press, 1964), 160 (no. 71).

3. See Theodore Richard DeWelles, "The Social and Political Content of the Towneley Cycle" (Ph.D. diss., University of Toronto, 1981), 61–62 and 120–21. DeWelles sees Cain as a typical yeoman, not specifically a Lollard, in his stance against tithing.

4. Hudson, *Selections*, 19.

5. Ibid., 21.

6. Gairdner, *Lollardy and the Reformation* 1:132.

7. Trevelyan, *Age of Wyclif*, 156.

8. See, e.g., Arnold, *Select English Works* 3:293–94.

9. P. L. Heyworth, ed., *Jack Upland, Friar Daw's Reply, and Upland's Rejoinder* (London: Oxford University Press, 1968), "Friar Daw's Reply," 74–75.

10. Ibid., "Upland's Rejoinder," 103.

11. Arnold, *Select English Works* 3:370–71.

12. Matthew, *English Works of Wyclif*, 37.

13. Ibid., 337.

14. See, for example, the opening line of "Jack Upland," in Heyworth, *Jack Upland*, 54: "To very God & to alle trewe in Crist"; see also the "Sixteen Points on which the Bishops accuse Lollards," wherein the accused Lollard is advised thus: "Trewe cristen men shulden answere here aviseliche, trewliche, and mekeliche" (Hudson, *Selections*, 20, and see 146, n. to line 50). Also relevant is Hudson, *Premature Reformation*, 10 (Lollards as "the community of *trewe men*") and 342.

15. Emphasis mine. Cited in G. R. Owst, *Preaching in Medieval England: An Introduction to Sermon Manuscripts of the Period 1350–1450* (Cambridge: Cambridge University Press, 1926), 174.

16. See Carl Horstmann, ed., *The Minor Poems of the Vernon MS*, Early

English Text Society (London: Kegan Paul, Trench, Trübner, 1892), pt. 1, 174, line 134; *The Minor Poems of John Lydgate*, ed. Henry Noble MacCracken, Early English Text Society (London: Kegan Paul, Trench, Trübner, 1911), 87, line 321.

Chapter 4. Priests and Polemics

1. *The Complete Works of John Gower*, ed. G. C. Macaulay (Oxford: Clarendon Press, 1902), 4:346–54.

2. Martin Stevens, "Language as Theme in the Wakefield Plays," *Speculum* 52 (1977): 103–4. As Stevens notes, Lucifer demonstrates "in the very form of his speech his incapacity to imitate God" (104); see also Stevens, *Four Middle English Mystery Cycles*, 160.

3. Stevens, *Four Middle English Mystery Cycles*, 156–69. The quotations are found on 156, 157, 169, 157, and 163.

4. Ibid., 170.

5. Ross, *Middle English Sermons*, 13.

6. DeWelles, "Social and Political Content," 353.

7. Rossell Hope Robbins, ed. *Historical Poems of the XIVth and XVth Centuries* (New York: Columbia University Press, 1959), 153, lines 12–24.

8. Heyworth, *Jack Upland*, 91, 97–98, and 102–13, passim.

9. Kendall, *Drama of Dissent*, 42. See also Kendall's analysis of the dramatic qualities of the *Jack Upland* series, 83–89, and Hudson, *Premature Reformation*, 220–24.

10. It should here be pointed out that the term *Lollard* for Wycliffite or heretic in general probably derives from the Dutch *lollen* (to mumble): see Hudson, *Selections*, 8. In the play's context, however, it can hardly have been intended to mean only "mumbler." See also Stevens, *Four Middle English Mystery Cycles*, 163n, for the suggestion that the Wakefield Master's use of the term here may reveal that he was himself a Wycliffite: "The word 'lollar' is used disparagingly by Tutivillus (374/213), but, given the source, that may indeed be high praise." However, as Tutivillus's disparagement is meant to be taken straightforwardly in general, I find it unlikely that the audience would have distinguished ironic intention in this one case.

11. See Kolve, *Play Called Corpus Christi*, 69.

12. Kendall, *Drama of Dissent*, 22. See also Tanner, *Heresy Trials*, 49 and 58; and Hudson, *Premature Reformation*, 322–23.

13. See Stevens, "Language as Theme," 110–11.

14. Kendall, *Drama of Dissent*, 18 and 43–44. That some women were indeed active and outspoken Lollards is evidenced in Tanner, *Heresy Trials*; see especially 41–51, 75, 138–44.

15. Priscilla Heath Barnum, ed., *Dives and Pauper*, part 1, Early English Text Society (London: Oxford University Press, 1976), 328.

16. Stevens, *Four Middle English Mystery Cycles*, 171.

17. Cited in Cawley, *Wakefield Pageants*, 98n.454. See also John Gardner, *The Construction of the Wakefield Cycle* (Carbondale and Edwardsville: Southern Illinois University Press, 1974), who sees this line as "calling up the idea of the feast of the blessed" (47).

18. See Kolve, *Play Called Corpus Christi*, 72–74.

19. See B. J. Kidd, *The Later Medieval Doctrine of the Eucharistic Sacrifice* (London: S.P.C.K., 1958), 28.

20. Hudson, *Selections*, 26.

21. See *Annunciacio*, 44, 128, 244; *Oblacio magorum*, 218, 223; *Pagina doctorum*, 26, 248; *Conspiracio*, 503, 523; *Processus crucis*, 351, 606; *Extraccio animarum*, 64, 254, 288.

22. Jungmann, *Mass of the Roman Rite* 2:65.

23. Ibid., 439–47.

24. See n.14 to chap. 1 above.

25. William Wolfe Capes, *The English Church in the Fourteenth and Fifteenth Centuries* (London: Macmillan, 1909), 124, 146.

26. See Walter E. Meyers, *A Figure Given: Typology in the Wakefield Plays* (Pittsburgh: Duquesne University Press, 1970), 36.

27. E. Catherine Dunn, "The Literary Style of the Towneley Plays," *American Benedictine Review* 20 (1969): 495.

28. Robert A. Brawer, "The Form and Function of the Prophetic Procession in the Middle English Cycle Play," *Annuale Mediaevale* 13 (1972): 119.

Chapter 5. The Word Incarnate: Infancy Plays

1. Theresa Coletti, "Devotional Iconography in the N-Town Marian Plays," *Comparative Drama* 11 (Spring 1977): 31. Coletti also notes the prominence of Eucharistic meanings in the Towneley shepherds' plays and suggests, "That the Wakefield Master saw fit to give extensive play to Eucharistic meanings at the dramatic moment of the Nativity certainly indicates that the dramatic audience would have been familiar with these meanings and further that they would have expected them" (32).

2. Leah Sinanoglou, "The Christ Child as Sacrifice: A Medieval Tradition and the Corpus Christi Plays," *Speculum* 48 (1973): 491.

3. In my discussion of the infancy plays I am dependent on Sinanoglou, "Christ Child as Sacrifice," for her analyses of the shepherds' plays (504–9) and the plays of the Purification (501–2). See also Travis, *Dramatic Design*, 111. On Lollard scorn for popular veneration of the elevated Host, see Hudson, *Premature Reformation*, 150.

4. I have discussed the relationship between the cycles and this tradition in "Middle English Elevation Prayers and the Corpus Christi Cycles," *English Language Notes* 17 (1979): 85–88. See also Richard J. Collier, *Poetry and Drama in the York Corpus Christi Play* (Hamden, Conn.: Shoe String Press, 1977), 141.

5. Simmons, *Lay Folks Mass Book*, 38, lines 401–411, 416–21.

6. See Rossell Hope Robbins, "Levation Prayers in Middle English Verse," *Modern Philology* 40 (1942): 131–46, for a discussion of the fifteen extant versified Middle English elevation prayers.

7. In "Sacrament and Sacrifice in the N-Town Passion," *Mediaevalia* 7 (1981): 239 and 257 n.1, Theresa Coletti catalogs a number of the Corpus Christi cycles' "allusions that identify Christ's human flesh with the Eucharistic sacrament," including "puns on 'foode,'" as well as the sheep-Child conflation in the *Secunda Pastorum*.

8. See Kolve, *Play Called Corpus Christi*, 172.

9. Rossell Hope Robbins, "Dissent in Middle English Literature: The Spirit of (Thirteen) Seventy-Six," *Medievalia et Humanistica*, n.s., 9 (1979): 38.

10. See 1 Cor. 1:24.

11. Maurice Vloberg, *L'Eucharistie dans l'art* (Grenoble and Paris: B. Arthaud, 1946), 173–75.

12. A. C. Cawley, "The 'Grotesque' Feast in the *Prima Pastorum*," *Speculum* 30 (1955): 215; William F. Munson, "Audience and Meaning in Two Medieval Dramatic Realisms," *Comparative Drama* 9 (1975): 59–60.

13. Margery M. Morgan, "'High Fraud': Paradox and Double-Plot in the English Shepherds' Plays," *Speculum* 39 (1964): 678–79.

14. Alicia K. Nitecki, "The Sacred Elements of the Secular Feast in *Prima Pastorum*," *Mediaevalia* 3 (1977): 229–37.

15. Lois Roney, "The Wakefield *First* and *Second Shepherds Plays* as Complements in Psychology and Parody," *Speculum* 58 (1983): 715–20.

16. On similar double entendres, see Morgan, "'High Fraud,'" 687.

17. Cawley, "'Grotesque' Feast," 215.

18. See Morgan, "'High Fraud,'" and Thomas J. Jambeck, "The 'Ayll of Hely' Allusion in the *Prima Pastorum*," *English Language Notes* 17 (1979): 1–7.

19. Horstmann, *Vernon MS*, pt. 1, 24.

20. See Meyers, *A Figure Given*, 67.

21. Jungmann, *Mass of the Roman Rite* 1:129; Sr. Loretta McGarry, *The Holy Eucharist in Middle English Homiletic and Devotional Verse* (Washington, D.C.: Catholic University of America, 1936), 87.

22. McGarry, *Holy Eucharist in Middle English Verse*, 117.

23. See DeWelles, "Social and Political Content," 357–58.

24. Cited in Workman, *John Wyclif* 2:204.

25. Cited in Owst, *Preaching*, 138–40.

26. Heyworth, *Jack Upland*, 85.

27. See, for example, Morgan, "'High Fraud,'" 686–87; William M. Manly, "Shepherds and Prophets: Religious Unity in the Towneley *Secunda Pastorum*," *PMLA* 78 (1963): 151–55; Linda E. Marshall, "'Sacral Parody' in the *Secunda Pastorum*," *Speculum* 47 (1972): 720–36.

28. Edward P. Cheyney, *The Dawn of a New Era, 1250–1453* (New York: Harper & Brothers, 1936), 222.

29. Sinanoglou, "Christ Child as Sacrifice," 508.

30. See Kolve, *Play Called Corpus Christi*, 45–50.

31. Marina Warner, *Alone of All Her Sex: The Myth and the Cult of the Virgin Mary* (New York: Alfred A. Knopf, 1976), 218.

32. See Jeffrey Helterman, *Symbolic Action in the Plays of the Wakefield Master* (Athens: University of Georgia Press, 1981), who demonstrates that Herod in this play celebrates a parody of the Mass that identifies him as Antichrist (130–36). This is by no means inconsistent with the possibility that Herod's characterization has a Lollard cast, especially in light of documented Lollard perversions of the Mass (see above, n.28).

33. See John Mirk, *Instructions for Parish Priests*, ed. Edward Peacock, Early English Text Society (London: Trübner, 1868), 9, lines 284–85.

34. Tanner, *Heresy Trials*, 81, 58; see also 49, 61.

Chapter 6. The Word Incarnate: Teachings and Sacrifice

1. Mirk, *Mirk's Festial*, 169.

2. Frederick E. Warren, trans., *The Sarum Missal in English*, Alcuin Club Collections, 11 (London: A. R. Mowbray, 1913), pt. 1, 362.

3. Warner, *Alone of All Her Sex*, 218.

4. See, e.g., Thomson, *Later Lollards*, 33–34.

5. Ibid., 41; see also 69.

6. Ibid., 127; see also Tanner, *Heresy Trials*, 10.

7. *Summa Theologiae*, vol. 58, 11–12, 3a73.3.

8. Rosemary Woolf, *The English Mystery Plays* (Berkeley and Los Angeles: University of California Press, 1972), 217.

9. See Mirk, *Instructions*, 10, lines 316–29, for a typical listing of the benefits derived from the sight of the consecrated Host.

10. See, however, Earl, "Shape of Old Testament History," 450–52, for an argument that the *Lazarus* was actually presented as the cycle's concluding play.

11. See Mirk, *Mirk's Festial*, 169.

12. Meg Twycross, " 'Apparell comlye,' " in *Aspects of Early English Drama*, ed. Paula Neuss (Cambridge: D. S. Brewer; Totowa, N.J.: Barnes & Noble, 1983), 44–45.

13. DeWelles, "Social and Political Content," 360–75.

14. Kendall, *Drama of Dissent*, 46. See also 55–67 on Lollard trials as "displaced drama."

15. Ibid., 405.

16. See Woolf, *English Mystery Plays*, 257; Stevens, "Language as Theme," 102, 111; Stevens, *Four Middle English Mystery Cycles*, 157.

17. Helterman, *Symbolic Action*, 139. See also DeWelles, "Social and Political Content," 405–6.

18. Migne, *Patrologia Latina*, vol. 169, col. 1470.

19. For a list of "virtues" including this, see Lydgate's "The Interpretation and Virtues of the Mass," in *Minor Poems*, 87–117.

20. See Tanner, *Heresy Trials*, 28, 45–46.

21. Mirk, *Instructions*, 10, lines 324–25.

22. Arnold Williams, *The Characterization of Pilate in the Towneley Plays* (East Lansing: Michigan State College Press, 1950), 27.

23. A. C. Cawley and Martin Stevens, "The Towneley *Processus Talentorum*: Text and Commentary," *Leeds Studies in English*, n.s., 17 (1986): 122.

24. Ibid.

25. Theresa Coletti, "Theology and Politics in the Towneley *Play of the Talents*," *Medievalia et Humanistica*, n.s., 9 (1979): 118–19.

26. See ibid., 114: "Without the knowledge that the Body of Christ remains one in spite of His death, the ending of the *Crucifixion* is potentially horrifying. The dramatic audience would know the joyous outcome of the Christian story; but the *Play of the Talents* serves to remind it of that outcome."

27. Woolf, *English Mystery Plays*, 268.

28. Coletti, "Theology and Politics," 113.

29. Cawley and Stevens, "Towneley *Processus Talentorum*," 124.

30. Woolf, *English Mystery Plays*, 271–72.

Chapter 7. Sacramental Fulfillment of the Word

1. Alan H. Nelson, *The Medieval English Stage: Corpus Christi Pageants and Plays* (Chicago and London: University of Chicago Press, 1974), 3.

2. See Trevelyan, *Age of Wyclif*, 293.

3. See, e.g., Hugh of Saint Victor, *On the Sacraments of the Christian Faith (De Sacramentis)*, trans. Roy J. Deferrari (Cambridge, Mass.: The Mediaeval Academy of America, 1951), 304–6.

4. Lawrence M. Clopper, ed., *Chester, Records of the Early English Drama*, vol. 3 (Toronto: University of Toronto Press, 1979), 245.

5. Matt. 26:26–29; Mark 14:22–25; Luke 22:17–20; 1 Cor. 11:23–26.

6. See Proctor and Wordsworth, *Breviarum*, vol. 1, col. 1068, in which a reading for the Feast of Corpus Christi supports this argument. It is appropriate that this feast be celebrated after Pentecost, for this is the time at which "Spiritus Sanctus discipulorum corda edocuit ad plene cognoscenda hujus mysteria sacramenti [the Holy Spirit instructed the disciples' hearts to full understanding of the mystery of that sacrament]."

7. See Woolf, *English Mystery Plays:* "Towneley here bases itself very closely on John, thus startlingly omitting the institution of the eucharist" (233).

8. Vloberg, *L'Eucharistie dans l'art*, 87.

9. See Netter, *Fasciculi Zizaniorum*, 167.

10. Pamela Sheingorn, "On Using Medieval Art in the Study of Medieval Drama: An Introduction to Methodology," *Research Opportunities in Renaissance Drama* 22 (1979): 105. See also Sheingorn's "The Moment of the Resurrection in the Corpus Christi Plays," *Medievalia et Humanistica*, n.s., 11 (1982): 111–29, where she discusses the gradual transfer—in response to the Anselmian atonement theory—of triumphant imagery from the depiction of the Crucifixion to that of the Resurrection.

11. Warren, *Sarum Missal*, pt. 1, 288–89.

12. Proctor and Wordsworth, *Breviarum*, vol. 1, col. 1098.

13. Sheingorn, "The Moment of the Resurrection," 121.

14. Meyers, *A Figure Given*, 96–97.

15. See Horstmann, *Vernon MS*, poems 30 and 31.

16. See J. W. Robinson, "The Late Medieval Cult of Jesus and the Mystery Plays," *PMLA* 80 (1965): 508–14. Robinson notes striking similarities between such scenes as this and the late medieval artistic motif of the Image of Pity. In both cases, Robinson suggests, the spectator "is in some kind of communion" (513) with the tortured, bleeding Christ.

17. Coletti, "Sacrament and Sacrifice," 248. See also 256, where Coletti describes the effect of Christ's reference to the Eucharist in the N-Town Resurrection scene.

18. Migne, *Patrologia Latina*, vol. 114, cols. 352–53.

19. Vloberg, *L'Eucharistie dans l'art*, 125–27.

20. Warren, *Sarum Missal*, pt. 1, 299.

21. Meyers, *A Figure Given*, 99–100.

22. *Summa Theologiae*, vol. 58, 116–19, 121–23.

23. McGarry, *Holy Eucharist in Middle English Verse*, 43; Jungmann, *Mass of the Roman Rite* 2:323–36.

24. Eleanor Prosser, *Drama and Religion in the English Mystery Plays: A Re-Evaluation* (Stanford, Calif.: Stanford University Press, 1961), 154.

25. Ibid.

26. Warren, *Sarum Missal*, pt. 1, 301–2.

27. See Saint Thomas Aquinas, *Summa Theologiae*, vol. 59, 6.

28. Prosser, *Drama and Religion*, 155.

29. Matt. 28:16–20; Mark 16:14–19; Acts 1:3–11.

30. Martin Stevens, "The Missing Parts of the Towneley Cycle," *Speculum* 45 (1970), 264.

31. Meyers, *A Figure Given*, 103.

32. Ibid., 102.

33. Ibid., 103.
34. Proctor and Wordsworth, *Breviarum*, vol. 1, col. 1067.

Chapter 8. Conclusion: The Last Mass

1. Woolf, *English Mystery Plays*, 71.
2. England and Pollard, *The Towneley Plays*, xx–xxi.
3. See Robinson, "Late Medieval Cult," 510.
4. Ibid., 512.
5. Clifford Davidson, "An Interpretation of the Wakefield *Judicium*," *Annuale Mediaevale* 10 (1969): 117.
6. *The Pricke of Conscience (Stimulus Conscientiae), A Northumbrian Poem by Richard Rolle de Hampole*, ed. Richard Morris (Berlin: A. Asher, 1863), 154, lines 5668–75.
7. Davidson, "Interpretation of *Judicium*," 112.
8. Ibid., 111.
9. Margaret Jennings, "Tutivillus: The Literary Career of the Recording Demon," *Studies in Philology* 74 (1977): 60. See also chap. 4 above, especially n. 10.
10. See Kolve, *Play Called Corpus Christi*, 282n.85.
11. Stevens, "Language as Theme," 108.
12. Rolle, *Pricke of Conscience*, 169–70, lines 6268–75.

Bibliography

Arnold, Thomas, ed. *Select English Works of John Wyclif.* 3 vols. Oxford: The Clarendon Press, 1869.

Aston, Margaret. *Lollards and Reformers: Images and Literacy in Late Medieval Religion.* London: The Hambledon Press, 1984.

Barish, Jonas. *The Antitheatrical Prejudice.* Berkeley: University of California Press, 1981.

Barnum, Priscilla Heath, ed. *Dives and Pauper.* Part 1. Early English Text Society. London: Oxford University Press, 1976.

Beadle, Richard, ed. *The York Plays.* London: Edward Arnold, 1982.

Bevington, David. *Medieval Drama.* Boston: Houghton Mifflin, 1975.

Bitts, Bing D. "The 'Suppression Theory' and the English Corpus Christi Play: A Re-Examination." *Theatre Journal* 32 (1980): 157–68.

Brawer, Robert A. "The Form and Function of the Prophetic Procession in the Middle English Cycle Play." *Annuale Mediaevale* 13 (1972): 88–124.

Brewer, J. S., ed. *Monumenta Franciscana.* London: Longman, Brown, Green, Longmans, and Roberts, 1858.

Bridgett, T. E. *A History of the Holy Eucharist in Great Britain.* London: T. Fisher Unwin, 1908.

Capes, William Wolfe. *The English Church in the Fourteenth and Fifteenth Centuries.* London: Macmillan, 1909.

Catto, J. I. "John Wyclif and the Cult of the Eucharist." In *The Bible in the Medieval World: Essays in Memory of Beryl Smalley,* edited by Katherine Walsh and Diana Wood. Oxford: published for the Ecclesiastical History Society by Basil Blackwell, 1985.

Cawley, A. C. "The 'Grotesque' Feast in the *Prima Pastorum.*" *Speculum* 30 (1955): 213–17.

———, ed. *The Wakefield Pageants in the Towneley Cycle.* Manchester: Manchester University Press, 1958.

Cawley, A. C., and Martin Stevens. "The Towneley *Processus Talentorum*: Text and Commentary." *Leeds Studies in English,* n.s., 17 (1986): 105–30.

Cawley, A. C., et al., eds. *The Revels History of Drama in English.* Vol. 1, *Medieval Drama.* London: Methuen, 1983.

Chambers, E. K. *The Medieval Stage.* 2 vols. London: Oxford University Press, 1903.

Chenu, M.-D. *Toward Understanding St. Thomas.* Translated by A.-M. Landry and D. Hughes. Chicago: Henry Regnery, 1964.

Cheyney, Edward P. *The Dawn of a New Era, 1250–1453.* New York: Harper & Brothers, 1936.

Clopper, Lawrence M., ed. *Chester.* Records of the Early English Drama, vol. 3. Toronto: University of Toronto Press, 1979.

Coletti, Theresa. "Devotional Iconography in the N-Town Marian Plays." *Comparative Drama* 11 (Spring 1979): 22–44.

———. "Sacrament and Sacrifice in the N-Town Passion." *Mediaevalia* 7 (1981): 239–64.

———. "Theology and Politics in the Towneley *Play of the Talents.*" *Medievalia et Humanistica*, n.s., 9 (1979): 111–26.

Collier, Richard J. *Poetry and Drama in the York Corpus Christi Play.* Hamden, Conn.: Shoe String Press, 1977.

Corblet, Jules. *Histoire dogmatique, liturgique et archéologique du sacrement de l'Eucharistie.* 2 vols. Paris: Société Générale de Librairie Catholique, 1885–86.

Cutts, Cecilia. "The Croxton Play: An Anti-Lollard Piece." *Modern Language Quarterly* 5 (1944): 45–60.

Davidson, Clifford. "An Interpretation of the Wakefield *Judicium.*" *Annuale Mediaevale* 10 (1969): 104–19.

———, ed. *A Middle English Treatise on the Playing of Miracles.* Washington, D.C.: University Press of America, 1981.

Davies, R. T., ed. *Medieval English Lyrics.* Chicago: Northwestern University Press, 1964.

Davis, Norman, ed. *Non-Cycle Plays and Fragments.* Early English Text Society. London: Oxford University Press, 1970.

Day, Mabel, ed. *The English Text of the Ancrene Riwle.* Early English Text Society. London: Oxford University Press, 1952.

Deanesly, Margaret. *The Lollard Bible and Other Medieval Biblical Versions.* Cambridge: Cambridge University Press, 1920.

DeWelles, Theodore Richard. "The Social and Political Content of the Towneley Cycle." Ph.D. diss., University of Toronto, 1981.

Dickens, A. G. *Lollards and Protestants in the Diocese of York, 1509–1558.* London and New York: published for the University of Hull by the Oxford University Press, 1959.

Drake, Francis. *Eboracum; or, The History and Antiquities of the City of York.* London: William Bowyer, 1736.

Dunn, E. Catherine. "The Literary Style of the Towneley Plays." *American Benedictine Review* 20 (1969): 481–504.

Earl, James W. "The Shape of Old Testament History in the Towneley Plays." *Studies in Philology* 69 (1972): 434–52.

England, George, and Alfred W. Pollard, eds. *The Towneley Plays.* Early English Text Society. 1897. Reprint. Millwood, N.Y.: Kraus, 1978.

Fines, John. "Studies in the Lollard Heresy. Being an Examination of the Evidence from the Dioceses of Norwich, Lincoln, Coventry and Lichfield, and Ely, during the period 1430–1530." Ph.D. diss., University of Sheffield, 1964.

Fletcher, Alan J. "John Mirk and the Lollards." *Medium Aevum* 56 (1987): 217–24.

Fox, Michael. "John Wyclif and the Mass." *Heythrop Journal* 3 (1962): 232–40.

Fraser, Russell. *The War against Poetry.* Princeton: Princeton University Press, 1970.

Gairdner, James. *Lollardy and the Reformation in England: An Historical Survey*. 2 vols. New York: Burt Franklin, 1908.

Gardiner, Harold C. *Mysteries' End*. 1946. Reprint. Hamden, Conn.: Archon, 1967.

Gardner, John. *The Construction of the Wakefield Cycle*. Carbondale and Edwardsville: Southern Illinois University Press, 1974.

Gower, John. *The Complete Works of John Gower*. Edited by G. C. Macaulay. 4 vols. Oxford: Clarendon Press, 1902.

Gradon, Pamela, ed. *English Wycliffite Sermons*. Vol. 2. Oxford: Clarendon Press, 1988.

Greene, Richard Leighton. *The Early English Carols*. Oxford: Clarendon Press, 1935.

Helterman, Jeffrey. *Symbolic Action in the Plays of the Wakefield Master*. Athens: University of Georgia Press, 1981.

Heyworth, P. L., ed. *Jack Upland, Friar Daw's Reply, and Upland's Rejoinder*. London: Oxford University Press, 1968.

Horstmann, Carl, ed. *The Minor Poems of the Vernon MS*. Early English Text Society. London: Kegan Paul, Trench, Trübner, 1892.

Hudson, Anne. *The Premature Reformation: Wycliffite Texts and Lollard History*. Oxford: Oxford University Press, 1988.

———, ed. *English Wycliffite Sermons*. Vol. 1. Oxford: Clarendon Press, 1983.

———, ed. *Selections from English Wycliffite Writings*. Cambridge: Cambridge University Press, 1978.

Hugh of St. Victor. *On the Sacraments of the Christian Faith (De Sacramentis)*. Translated by Roy J. Deferrari. Cambridge, Mass.: The Mediaeval Academy of America, 1951.

Jambeck, Thomas J. "The 'Ayll of Hely' Allusion in the *Prima Pastorum*." *English Language Notes* 17 (1979): 1–7.

James, Mervyn. "Ritual, Drama and Social Body in the Late Medieval English Town." *Past and Present* 98 (February 1983): 3–29.

Jennings, Margaret. "Tutivillus: The Literary Career of the Recording Demon." *Studies in Philology* 74 (1977): 1–95.

Jones, W. R. "Lollards and Images: The Defense of Religious Art in Later Medieval England." *Journal of the History of Ideas* 34 (1973): 27–50.

Jungmann, Rev. Joseph A. *The Mass of the Roman Rite (Missarum Sollemnia)*. 2 vols. New York: Benziger Brothers, 1951.

Kendall, Ritchie D. *The Drama of Dissent: The Radical Poetics of Nonconformity, 1380–1590*. Chapel Hill: University of North Carolina Press, 1986.

Kidd, B. J. *The Later Medieval Doctrine of the Eucharistic Sacrifice*. London: S.P.C.K., 1958.

Kightly, Charles. "The Early Lollards: A Survey of Popular Lollard Activity in England, 1382–1428." Ph.D. diss., University of York, 1975.

Kolve, V. A. *The Play Called Corpus Christi*. Stanford, Calif.: Stanford University Press, 1966.

Lepow, Lauren. "The Contrasted Courts in *Sir Gawain and the Green Knight*." In *The Medieval Court in Europe*, edited by Edward R. Haymes, 200–208. Houston German Studies 6. Munich: Wilhelm Fink Verlag, 1986.

———. "Drama of Communion: The Life of Christ in the Towneley Cycle."
Philological Quarterly 62 (1983): 403–13.

———. "Middle English Elevation Prayers and the Corpus Christi Cycles."
English Language Notes 17 (1979): 85–88.

Love, Nicholas, trans. *The Mirrour of the Blessed Lyf of Jesu Christ*. Edited by
Lawrence F. Powell. Oxford: Clarendon Press, 1908.

Lumby, Joseph Rawson, ed. *Chronicon Henrici Knighton*. 2 vols. London, 1889.

Lydgate, John. *The Minor Poems of John Lydgate*. Edited by Henry Noble
MacCracken. Early English Text Society. London: Kegan Paul, Trench,
Trübner, 1911.

McGarry, Sr. Loretta. *The Holy Eucharist in Middle English Homiletic and
Devotional Verse*. Washington, D.C.: Catholic University of America, 1936.

McGoldrick, James Edward. "Patrick Hamilton, Luther's Scottish Disciple." *The
Sixteenth Century Journal* 18 (1987): 81–88.

Manly, William M. "Shepherds and Prophets: Religious Unity in the Towneley
Secunda Pastorum." *PMLA* 78 (1963): 151–55.

Marshall, Linda E. " 'Sacral Parody' in the *Secunda Pastorum*." *Speculum* 47
(1972): 720–36.

Matthew, F. D., ed. *The English Works of Wyclif Hitherto Unprinted*. Early
English Text Society. London: Kegan Paul, Trench, Trübner, 1880.

Meyers, Walter E. *A Figure Given: Typology in the Wakefield Plays*. Pittsburgh:
Duquesne University Press, 1970.

Migne, J. P., ed. *Patrologiae Cursus Completus: Series Latina*. 221 vols. Paris,
1844–64.

Mills, David. " 'The Towneley Plays' or 'The Towneley Cycle'?" *Leeds Studies
in English*, n.s, 17 (1986): 95–104.

Mirk, John. *Instructions for Parish Priests*. Edited by Edward Peacock. Early
English Text Society. London: Trübner, 1868.

———. *Mirk's Festial: A Collection of Homilies by Johannis Mirkus (John Mirk)*.
Edited by Theodor Erbe. Early English Text Society. London: Kegan Paul,
Trench, Trübner, 1905.

Morgan, Margery. " 'High Fraud': Paradox and Double-Plot in the English Shepherds' Plays." *Speculum* 39 (1964): 676–89.

Morin, Germain. *Etudes, textes, découverts: contributions à la littérature et à
l'histoire des douze premiers siècles*. 2 vols. Paris: A. Picard, 1913.

Mueller, Janel M. *The Native Tongue and the Word: Developments in English
Prose Style 1380–1580*. Chicago and London: University of Chicago Press,
1984.

Munson, William F. "Audience and Meaning in Two Medieval Dramatic Realisms." *Comparative Drama* 9 (1975): 44–67.

Nelson, Alan H. *The Medieval English Stage: Corpus Christi Pageants and
Plays*. Chicago and London: University of Chicago Press, 1974.

Netter, Thomas [Waldensis]. *Doctrinale Antiquitatem Fidei Catholicae Ecclesiae. De Sacramentalibus*. 1759. Reprint. Plymouth, Mich.: Gregg Press, 1967.

———[?]. *Fasciculi Zizaniorum Magistri Johannis Wyclif Cum Tritico*. Edited
by Walter Waddington Shirley. London: Longman, Brown, Green, Longmans,
and Roberts, 1858.

Nitecki, Alicia K. "The Sacred Elements of the Secular Feast in *Prima Pastorum*." *Mediaevalia* 3 (1977): 229–37.

Owst, G. R. *Literature and Pulpit in Medieval England*. 1933. Reprint. New York: Barnes & Noble, 1966.

———. *Preaching in Medieval England: An Introduction to Sermon Manuscripts of the Period 1350–1450*. Cambridge: Cambridge University Press, 1926.

Proctor, Francis, and Christopher Wordsworth, eds. *Breviarum ad usum insignis ecclesiae Sarum*. 2 vols. Cambridge, 1882.

Prosser, Eleanor. *Drama and Religion in the English Mystery Plays: A Re-Evaluation*. Stanford, Calif.: Stanford University Press, 1961.

Robbins, Rossell Hope. "Dissent in Middle English Literature: The Spirit of (Thirteen) Seventy-Six." *Medievalia et Humanistica*, n.s., 9 (1979): 25–51.

———. "Levation Prayers in Middle English Verse." *Modern Philology* 40 (1942): 131–46.

———, ed. *Historical Poems of the XIVth and XVth Centuries*. New York: Columbia University Press, 1959.

Robinson, J. W. "The Late Medieval Cult of Jesus and the Mystery Plays." *PMLA* 80 (1965): 508–14.

Rolle, Richard. *The Pricke of Conscience (Stimulus Conscientiae). A Northumbrian Poem by Richard Rolle de Hampole*. Edited by Richard Morris. Berlin: A. Asher, 1863.

Roney, Lois. "The Wakefield *First* and *Second Shepherds Plays* as Complements in Psychology and Parody." *Speculum* 58 (1983): 715–20.

Ross, Woodburn O., ed. *Middle English Sermons*. Early English Text Society. London: Oxford University Press, 1960.

Sheingorn, Pamela. "The Moment of Resurrection in the Corpus Christi Plays." *Medievalia et Humanistica*, n.s., 11 (1982): 111–29.

———. "On Using Medieval Art in the Study of Medieval Drama: An Introduction to Methodology." *Research Opportunities in Renaissance Drama* 22 (1979): 101–9.

Simmons, Thomas Frederick, ed. *The Lay Folks Mass Book*. Early English Text Society. 1879. Reprint. London: Oxford University Press, 1968.

Sinanoglou, Leah. "The Christ Child as Sacrifice: A Medieval Tradition and the Corpus Christi Plays." *Speculum* 48 (1973): 491–509.

Stevens, Martin. *Four Middle English Mystery Cycles: Textual, Contextual, and Critical Interpretations*. Princeton: Princeton University Press, 1987.

———. "Language as Theme in the Wakefield Plays." *Speculum* 52 (1977): 100–117.

———. "The Missing Parts of the Towneley Cycle." *Speculum* 45 (1970): 254–65.

Stone, Darwell. *A History of the Doctrine of the Holy Eucharist*. London: Longmans, Green, 1909.

Swinburn, Lilian M., ed. *The Lanterne of Liȝt*. Early English Text Society. London: Kegan Paul, Trench, Trübner, 1917.

Tanner, Norman P., ed. *Heresy Trials in the Diocese of Norwich, 1428–31*. Camden Fourth Series, vol. 20. London: Royal Historical Society, 1977.

Taylor, Jerome, and Alan Nelson, eds. *Medieval English Drama: Essays Critical and Contextual.* Chicago: University of Chicago Press, 1972.

Thomas Aquinas, Saint. *Summa Theologiae: Latin Text and English Translation.* 60 vols. New York: McGraw Hill, 1964–75.

Thomson, John A. F. *The Later Lollards, 1414–1520.* London: Oxford University Press, 1965.

Travis, Peter W. *Dramatic Design in the Chester Cycle.* Chicago: University of Chicago Press, 1982.

Trevelyan, George Macaulay. *England in the Age of Wycliffe, 1368–1520.* 1899. Reprint. New York: Harper & Row, 1963.

Tricomi, Albert H., ed. *Early Drama to 1600.* Acta (Proceedings of SUNY Regional Conferences in Medieval Studies), vol. 13. Binghamton: Center for Medieval and Early Renaissance Studies, State University of New York at Binghamton, 1987.

Twycross, Meg. " 'Apparell comlye.' " In *Aspects of Early English Drama,* edited by Paula Neuss, 30–49. Cambridge: D. S. Brewer; Totowa, N.J.: Barnes & Noble, 1983.

Vloberg, Maurice. *L'Eucharistie dans l'art.* Grenoble and Paris: B. Arthaud, 1946.

Warner, Marina. *Alone of All Her Sex: The Myth and the Cult of the Virgin Mary.* New York: Alfred A. Knopf, 1976.

Warren, Frederick E., trans. *The Sarum Missal in English.* Alcuin Club Collections, 11. London: A. R. Mowbray, 1913.

Williams, Arnold. *The Characterization of Pilate in the Towneley Plays.* East Lansing: Michigan State College Press, 1950.

Winn, Herbert E., ed. *Wyclif: Select English Writings.* 1929. Reprint. New York: AMS Press, 1976.

Woolf, Rosemary. *The English Mystery Plays.* Berkeley and Los Angeles: University of California Press, 1972.

Workman, Herbert B. *John Wyclif: A Study of the English Medieval Church.* 2 vols. 1926. Reprint. Hamden, Conn.: Archon, 1966.

[Wyclif, John?] *Wycklyffes Wicket.* 1546. Reprint. Oxford: Oxford University Press, 1828.

Wylie, James Hamilton. *History of England under Henry the Fourth.* 4 vols. London: Longmans, Green, 1896.

Index

"Sixteen Points on which the Bishops accuse Lollards," 57

Sorcery, 89

Stevens, Martin, 47, 51, 56, 71, 102, 111–12, 146 n.2, 151 n.1, 152 nn. 2 and 10

Taylor, Jerome, 43

Tertullian, 14

Thomas Aquinas, Saint, 29, 42–43, 100, 125

Thomson, John A. F., 22–23

Thorpe, William, 22, 36

Tithing, 22, 23, 56–57, 59, 60, 75

Tolkien, J. R. R., 72

Travis, Peter, 28, 50, 52

Tretise of Miraclis Pleyinge, A, 14, 15, 27

Trevelyan, George Macaulay, 22, 36, 58

Tricomi, Albert H., 145 n.3

"Twelve Conclusions of the Lollards," 24

Twycross, Meg, 103

"Verbum supernum prodiens," 42

"Virtues" of the Mass, 88, 109, 113, 155 n.19

Wakefield Master, 14, 51, 55, 65, 67, 83, 88, 94, 105, 137, 139, 141, 143–44, 151 n.68

Whitehorne, John, 36

Williams, Arnold, 111

Woolf, Rosemary, 100, 112, 114, 137, 156 n.7

Workman, Herbert B., 36

Wycklyffes Wycket, 36

Wyclif, John, 12, 21–22, 23, 31–32, 33–34, 64, 83, 140, 147 n.22; on conscience, 59; on disendowment, 21; on dominion by grace, 21; on drama, 26; on "fables," 25; on guilds, 26, 29; on images, 24–25; on music, 26; on preaching, 36–37; on work, 58

York cycle, 28, 51, 96, 116, 127, 137, 146 n.7

York Diocese, 22, 23, 47